EDINB
TRAVEL GI
AND BE

CW00496306

Your Ultimate Handbook to Exploring the Heart of
Scotland

Lewis Noah

CONTENTS

INTRODUCTION

Welcome to the ultimate handbook for exploring Edinburgh, the heart of Scotland! Whether you're planning a trip in 2024 or beyond, this travel guide is here to provide you with all the information you need to make the most of your visit to this captivating city. Edinburgh is a place where history meets modernity, where stunning architecture coexists with vibrant cultural festivals, and where the beauty of the Scottish landscape is just a stone's throw away. From the iconic Edinburgh Castle to the charming streets of the Old Town and the bustling atmosphere of the Royal Mile, there is something for everyone in this enchanting city. So, get ready to immerse yourself in the rich heritage, cultural experiences, and breathtaking landscapes that Edinburgh has to offer!

BACKGROUND INFORMATION

History & Origin

he history of Edinburgh dates back thousands of years. The T earliest evidence of human settlement in the area dates to around 8500 BC, with the discovery of Mesolithic artifacts. The area was later inhabited by the Celtic people known as the Votadini, and it became an important hillfort called Din Eidyn.

In the 7th century, the area came under the control of the Angles, a Germanic tribe, and was known as Edwin's Burgh, named after King Edwin of Northumbria. The town grew in prominence during the Middle Ages and became the capital of Scotland in the 15th century.

During the 16th and 17th centuries, Edinburgh played a significant role in the Scottish Reformation and became a center of intellectual and cultural development known as the Scottish Enlightenment. Many prominent figures of the time, such as philosopher David Hume and economist Adam Smith, lived and worked in Edinburgh, making it a hub of intellectual activity.

Edinburgh's history is marked by political and religious conflicts. The city saw several sieges and battles, including the Wars of Scottish Independence in the 13th and 14th centuries. The most famous event was the Battle of Flodden in 1513, where King James IV of Scotland was killed.

The city's architecture reflects its rich history. The Old Town and New Town of Edinburgh, both UNESCO World Heritage Sites, showcase distinct architectural styles. The Old Town is characterized by its narrow, winding medieval streets, while the New Town features elegant Georgian buildings and spacious squares.

Today, Edinburgh is the capital city of Scotland and a major cultural, educational, and economic center. It continues to attract visitors from around the world who come to explore its historic landmarks, vibrant festivals, and thriving arts scene.

Culture & Customs

Edinburgh, the capital city of Scotland, is known for its rich cultural heritage and vibrant customs. Here are some key aspects of Edinburgh's culture and customs:

Festivals

Edinburgh is famous for hosting a variety of festivals throughout the year. The most renowned is the Edinburgh Festival Fringe, the world's largest arts festival, which takes place in August. Other notable festivals include the Edinburgh International Festival, Edinburgh International Book Festival, and the Hogmanay (New Year's) celebrations.

Scottish Traditions

Edinburgh embraces and celebrates Scottish traditions, including bagpipe music, Highland dancing, and traditional Scottish attire such as kilts and tartans. The city has numerous Highland Games events, where you can witness competitions like caber tossing, hammer throwing, and Highland dancing.

Architecture

Edinburgh's architecture is a blend of medieval, Georgian, and Victorian styles. The iconic Edinburgh Castle, located on Castle Rock, dominates the city's skyline. The Royal Mile, a historic street that stretches from the castle to the Palace of Holyroodhouse, is lined with centuries-old buildings and landmarks.

Literary Heritage

Edinburgh has a rich literary history, being the birthplace of famous writers like Sir Walter Scott, Robert Louis Stevenson, and Sir Arthur Conan Doyle. The city has many literary landmarks, including the Writers' Museum, dedicated to Scottish literature, and the Scott Monument, a Victorian Gothic monument honoring Sir Walter Scott.

Pub Culture

Like the rest of Scotland, Edinburgh has a thriving pub culture. Pubs are social hubs where locals and visitors gather to enjoy traditional Scottish food, drinks like Scotch whisky, and live music sessions. The pub atmosphere is warm and welcoming, providing an opportunity to engage in conversations and experience Scottish hospitality.

Royal Connections

Edinburgh has strong ties to the British royal family. The Palace of Holyroodhouse, the official residence of the Queen in Scotland, is located at the eastern end of the Royal Mile. The annual Royal Edinburgh Military Tattoo, held at Edinburgh Castle, showcases military bands and performances from around the world.

Ceilidhs

Ceilidhs are traditional Scottish social gatherings that involve music, dancing, and storytelling. In Edinburgh, you can find ceilidh events where both locals and tourists come together to enjoy lively music, energetic dances like the Dashing White Sergeant and Strip the Willow, and the lively spirit of Scottish culture.

Ghost Stories and Supernatural Tales

Edinburgh is known for its spooky history and ghostly legends. The city's underground vaults and narrow closes (alleyways) are said to be haunted, and ghost tours offer the opportunity to explore these eerie tales. The annual Samhuinn Fire Festival, held around Halloween, celebrates the Celtic New Year with a theatrical and supernatural-themed procession.

Geographical Features

Edinburgh, the capital city of Scotland, is known for its stunning geographical features that contribute to its unique charm and beauty. Here are some of the notable geographical features of Edinburgh:

Arthur's Seat

Located in Holyrood Park, Arthur's Seat is an extinct volcano that offers breathtaking views of the city. Standing at 251 meters (823 feet) high, it is a popular spot for hiking, picnicking, and enjoying nature.

Castle Rock

Edinburgh Castle, one of the city's most iconic landmarks, sits atop Castle Rock. This ancient volcanic rock formation rises approximately 130 meters (430 feet) above sea level and provides panoramic views of the city.

Calton Hill

Situated in the city center, Calton Hill is a prominent hill with various monuments and landmarks. It offers panoramic views of the cityscape, including Edinburgh Castle, Holyrood Palace, and the Scottish Parliament.

Water of Leith

The Water of Leith is a river that flows through Edinburgh, adding to the city's natural beauty. It stretches approximately 35 kilometers (22 miles) and provides opportunities for leisurely walks and wildlife spotting.

Firth of Forth

Edinburgh lies on the southern shore of the Firth of Forth, an estuary of the River Forth. The Firth of Forth is known for its iconic Forth Bridges, including the Forth Rail Bridge, Forth Road Bridge, and Queensferry Crossing.

Pentland Hills

Located to the south of the city, the Pentland Hills form a picturesque range of rolling hills and moorland. They offer opportunities for hiking, cycling, and enjoying the outdoors.

Holyrood Park

Situated at the foot of Arthur's Seat, Holyrood Park is a vast green space that encompasses diverse landscapes, including grassy slopes, rocky outcrops, and a loch. It is a popular area for walking, jogging, and enjoying outdoor activities.

Portobello Beach

Edinburgh is also fortunate to have a beautiful sandy beach known as Portobello Beach. Located on the eastern outskirts of the city, it stretches along the Firth of Forth and provides a scenic coastal area for leisurely walks and recreational activities.

Traditional Edinburgh music and dance

Traditional Edinburgh music and dance are an integral part of the city's cultural heritage. Here are some notable forms of traditional music and dance in Edinburgh:

Scottish Country Dancing

Scottish country dancing is a social dance form that originated in Scotland. It involves sets of couples dancing various formations to traditional Scottish music. In Edinburgh, you can find regular Scottish country dance events and classes where locals and visitors can learn and participate in this lively dance form.

Ceilidh Dancing

Ceilidh (pronounced "kay-lee") dancing is another popular traditional dance form in Edinburgh. Ceilidhs are informal social gatherings that feature live traditional music and energetic group dancing. Common ceilidh dances include the Dashing White Sergeant, Strip the Willow, and the Gay Gordons. Ceilidhs are held at various venues throughout the city and are a great way to experience the joy and camaraderie of Scottish dance.

Bagpipe Music

The sound of bagpipes is synonymous with Scottish music. Edinburgh has a strong bagpipe tradition, and you can often hear bagpipers playing on the Royal Mile or during special events and ceremonies. The annual Royal Edinburgh Military Tattoo, held at Edinburgh Castle, showcases impressive bagpipe performances by military bands from Scotland and around the world.

Traditional Folk Music

Edinburgh has a thriving folk music scene that embraces traditional Scottish music. Folk musicians often perform in pubs and music venues across the city, playing instruments like fiddles, guitars, accordions, and bodhrans. These performances feature traditional

Scottish tunes, ballads, and songs that celebrate Scottish culture and history.

Edinburgh Folk Club

The Edinburgh Folk Club is a renowned venue for traditional folk music in the city. Established in 1973, it hosts regular folk music concerts, featuring local and international artists. The club provides a platform for both established and emerging folk musicians, contributing to the preservation and promotion of traditional music in Edinburgh.

Traditional Instruments

Edinburgh's traditional music often incorporates various instruments. In addition to bagpipes, you may hear the fiddle (violin), accordion, Scottish harp, bodhran (drum), and the Scottish smallpipes. These instruments are integral to the authentic sound of traditional Scottish music and contribute to the vibrant music scene in Edinburgh.

Edinburgh Folk Festival

The Edinburgh Folk Festival is an annual event that celebrates traditional and contemporary folk music. The festival brings together renowned folk artists for concerts, workshops, and sessions held in various venues across the city. It is a great opportunity to immerse yourself in the richness of Scottish folk music.

Edinburgh Language

Edinburgh, being the capital city of Scotland, has a linguistic landscape that reflects the diverse language heritage of the country. While the predominant language spoken in Edinburgh is English, there are also regional languages, including Scots and Gaelic, that contribute to the linguistic tapestry of the city. Here's an overview of Scots and Gaelic in Edinburgh:

Scots Language

Scots is a Germanic language closely related to English and has a long history in Scotland. It has its own distinct vocabulary, pronunciation, and grammatical features. In Edinburgh, you may hear the Scots language being spoken, particularly in more informal or colloquial settings. Scots has influenced the local dialect and is often used in expressions, idioms, and place names throughout the city.

Gaelic Language

Gaelic, also known as Scottish Gaelic, is a Celtic language and one of the indigenous languages of Scotland. It is primarily spoken in the Highlands and Islands, but there is also a Gaelic-speaking community in Edinburgh. While the number of Gaelic speakers in the city is relatively small, there are efforts to promote and preserve the language through Gaelic -medium education and cultural initiatives. The Scottish Parliament also provides bilingual services in English and Gaelic.

Signage and Place Names

In Edinburgh, you can find signage and place names that incorporate both Scots and Gaelic. For example, street names, landmarks, and institutions often have names in Scots or Gaelic alongside their English counterparts. This reflects the city's commitment to recognizing and celebrating its linguistic diversity.

Language Revitalization

In recent years, there has been a growing awareness and support for the revitalization of Scots and Gaelic languages in Edinburgh and across Scotland. Efforts are being made to encourage language learning, promote cultural events, and provide resources for those interested in studying and using these languages.

Iconic symbols

Edinburgh, as the capital city of Scotland, has several iconic symbols that represent its history, culture, and identity. Here are some of the most notable iconic symbols of Edinburgh:

Edinburgh Castle

Perched atop Castle Rock, Edinburgh Castle is perhaps the most recognizable symbol of the city. Its historic significance, commanding presence, and stunning architecture make it an iconic landmark. The castle has stood for centuries and is now a popular tourist attraction, offering panoramic views of the city.

Tartan and Kilts

Tartan is a patterned textile design that holds great significance in Scottish culture. Kilts, made from tartan fabric, are traditional Scottish garments often associated with Edinburgh and Scotland as a whole. The sight of people wearing kilts, especially during cultural events or festivals, is a symbol of Scottish heritage.

Royal Mile

The Royal Mile is a historic street that stretches from Edinburgh Castle to the Palace of Holyroodhouse. It is lined with medieval and Georgian buildings, bustling shops, restaurants, and attractions. The Royal Mile represents the heart of Edinburgh's Old Town and is a significant symbol of the city's rich history and royal connections.

Arthur's Seat

Located in Holyrood Park, Arthur's Seat is an ancient volcano and natural landmark in Edinburgh. Its distinctive shape and panoramic views make it an iconic symbol of the city. Arthur's Seat offers a popular hiking and walking destination, providing both locals and visitors with a tranquil escape and stunning vistas of Edinburgh.

Scott Monument

The Scott Monument is a Victorian Gothic monument dedicated to the renowned Scottish writer Sir Walter Scott. Located in Princes Street Gardens, it stands as the largest monument to a writer in the world. Its intricate design and towering presence make it a distinctive symbol of Edinburgh's literary heritage.

Thistle

The thistle is the national emblem of Scotland and is deeply ingrained in Scottish identity. It is often depicted in Edinburgh's architecture, artwork, and decorative elements, symbolizing resilience, pride, and the country's natural beauty.

Bagpipes

Bagpipes are synonymous with Scottish culture, and their presence is often associated with Edinburgh. The sound of bagpipes can be heard along the Royal Mile or during special events and ceremonies. Bagpipes are an iconic symbol of Scottish traditions and add to the cultural identity of Edinburgh.

The Edinburgh Enlightenment

The Edinburgh Enlightenment refers to a significant intellectual and cultural movement that took place in Edinburgh, Scotland, during the 18th century. It was a period of remarkable progress in various fields, including philosophy, science, literature, medicine, and social reform. The Edinburgh Enlightenment played a crucial role in shaping modern Scotland and influencing intellectual thought worldwide. Here are key aspects of the Edinburgh Enlightenment:

Intellectual Gathering

Edinburgh became a hub for intellectuals, scholars, and philosophers who gathered to exchange ideas and engage in intellectual discourse. Salons, coffeehouses, and universities like the University of Edinburgh served as meeting places for these thinkers, fostering a vibrant intellectual community.

Enlightenment Philosophy

The Edinburgh Enlightenment embraced the ideals of the broader European Enlightenment movement, emphasizing reason, skepticism, and the pursuit of knowledge. Scottish philosophers such as David Hume, Adam Smith, and Thomas Reid made significant contributions to fields like moral philosophy, political economy, and epistemology.

Moral and Political Philosophy

The Edinburgh Enlightenment produced influential works in moral and political philosophy. Adam Smith's "The Theory of Moral Sentiments" explored the concept of sympathy and laid the foundation for his later work on economics, "The Wealth of Nations." The ideas of social equality, individual liberty, and the pursuit of happiness were central to the moral and political philosophy of the time.

Science and Medicine

Edinburgh became a center for scientific and medical advancements during the Enlightenment. The University of Edinburgh played a vital role in promoting scientific research and education. Notable figures like Joseph Black, James Hutton, and James Clerk Maxwell made groundbreaking contributions to fields such as chemistry, geology, and physics.

Encyclopedism and Enlightenment Literature

The Scottish Enlightenment also saw a surge in literary and intellectual publications. The Encyclopaedia Britannica, first published in Edinburgh in 1768, became a significant source of knowledge and an embodiment of Enlightenment ideals. Scottish writers, including Robert Burns and Walter Scott, emerged during this period, contributing to Scottish literature and folklore.

Social Reform

The thinkers of the Edinburgh Enlightenment were often driven by a desire to improve society. They advocated for educational reform, prison reform, and improvements in healthcare and public welfare. The focus on practical improvements and social progress was a notable feature of the Edinburgh Enlightenment.

Legacy

The intellectual legacy of the Edinburgh Enlightenment had a lasting impact on Scotland and beyond. The ideas and innovations that emerged during this period helped shape modern disciplines and influenced subsequent intellectual movements. Edinburgh's reputation as a center for intellectual excellence continued to thrive, and the city remains a vibrant hub of education, culture, and innovation.

Literary and Cultural Significance

Edinburgh holds significant literary and cultural importance, serving as a hub of creativity, intellectual discourse, and artistic expression. The city's rich literary heritage and vibrant cultural scene have contributed to its international reputation. Here are some key aspects of Edinburgh's literary and cultural significance:

Literary Greats

Edinburgh has been home to renowned literary figures who have made enduring contributions to world literature. Authors such as Sir Walter Scott, Robert Burns, Robert Louis Stevenson, and Sir Arthur Conan Doyle were either born in Edinburgh or spent significant periods of their lives in the city. Their works, ranging from historical novels to poetry and detective fiction, continue to captivate readers worldwide.

Edinburgh as a Literary Setting

The city's historic and atmospheric streets, architecture, and landscapes have served as inspiration for numerous works of literature. Edinburgh's Old Town and Royal Mile, in particular, have been featured in countless novels, providing a rich backdrop for stories set in different time periods and genres.

Edinburgh International Book Festival

The Edinburgh International Book Festival is a major annual event that celebrates literature and brings together acclaimed authors, poets, and thinkers from around the world. It offers a platform for literary discussions, book launches, readings, and workshops, attracting literary enthusiasts and fostering a love for reading and writing.

Scottish Storytelling Tradition

Edinburgh has a strong tradition of storytelling, rooted in Scotland's oral heritage. From ancient folklore and myths to modern storytelling events, Edinburgh hosts numerous storytelling festivals and gatherings that highlight the power of spoken word and the art of storytelling.

UNESCO City of Literature

In 2004, Edinburgh was designated as the world's first UNESCO City of Literature, recognizing its historical and contemporary literary achievements. This prestigious title acknowledges the city's commitment to promoting literature, supporting writers, and fostering cultural exchange through literature.

Festivals and Cultural Events

Edinburgh's festivals are renowned worldwide and contribute significantly to its cultural significance. The Edinburgh Festival Fringe, Edinburgh International Festival, Edinburgh International Book Festival, and the Hogmanay celebrations attract artists, performers, and visitors from all corners of the globe, creating a vibrant atmosphere of creativity and cultural exchange.

Museums and Literary Landmarks

Edinburgh is home to various museums and landmarks that celebrate its literary heritage. The Writers' Museum pays tribute to Scotland's literary greats, while the Scott Monument and the Robert Burns Birthplace Museum honor the works and legacies of Sir Walter Scott and Robert Burns, respectively. These sites provide visitors with insights into the lives and works of these influential writers.

Art Galleries and Theatres

Edinburgh boasts a thriving art scene, with numerous art galleries, theaters, and performance venues. The Scottish National Gallery, the National Museum of Scotland, and the Edinburgh Playhouse are among the notable cultural institutions that showcase visual arts, theater productions, and live performances, adding to the city's cultural richness.

Influence of Edinburgh Clans

While Edinburgh is not traditionally associated with specific clans in the same way as other parts of Scotland, the city has historical connections to various clans that have influenced its culture and history. Here are a few notable clans and their influence on Edinburgh:

Clan Stewart

The Stewart or Stuart clan has strong historical ties to Edinburgh. The Royal House of Stewart, which originated in Scotland, held significant influence over the city and the country for centuries. Edinburgh Castle, a prominent landmark in the city, was often associated with the Stewarts, who used it as a royal residence.

Clan Douglas

The powerful Clan Douglas played a crucial role in the history of Edinburgh. The Black Douglas, led by Sir James Douglas, had a formidable presence in the city during the 14th century. The Douglas family held the title of Earl of Morton and exerted political influence in Edinburgh and beyond.

Clan Campbell

While primarily associated with the Argyll region, Clan Campbell had an impact on Edinburgh's history. The Campbell clan rose to prominence during the 15th and 16th centuries and held positions of power in Scotland. Archibald Campbell, the Marquess of Argyll, played a significant role in Edinburgh during the tumultuous events of the 17th century.

Clan Macdonald

The Clan Macdonald, particularly the MacDonalds of Sleat, had a presence in Edinburgh. During the 18th century, they were influential landowners and played a role in the cultural and political life of the city.

Clan Sinclair

Clan Sinclair, associated with the Castle of Roslin near Edinburgh, has historical connections to the city. The St. Clair family, the chiefs of the Sinclair clan, held the title of Earl of Orkney and played a part in the governance of Edinburgh.

STARTING YOUR TRIP

E dinburgh, the capital city of Scotland, is a vibrant and historic destination that offers a perfect blend of ancient landmarks, cultural attractions, and stunning natural beauty. If you're starting your trip to Edinburgh, here's a travel guide to help you make the most of your visit.

Why Go To Edinburgh

Burrowed beside long-dormant volcanoes and reigning over green moorlands, Edinburgh (or Ed-n-bruh in Scots speech) is known for more than its staggering landscape. The Athens of the North, as Edinburgh is sometimes nicknamed, also claims a cast of near-mythic characters: Rebel leader Sir William Wallace (aka Braveheart); the tragic Mary, Queen of Scots; the Enlightenment thinkers David Hume and Adam Smith; "James Bond" actor Sean Connery; and prolific wordsmiths Sir Arthur Conan Doyle and J.K. Rowling – are all woven into this very old, yet very relevant city.

But if your impression is confined to bagpipes, tartans, crests and kilts, you'd be wrong. The second most-visited city in the United Kingdom (after London), Edinburgh offers an abundance of things to do. History buffs will enjoy Edinburgh Castle, Holyroodhouse Palace and other attractions found along the Royal Mile. Those in search of an authentic live-as-the-locals experience will find it in the outer-lying neighborhood pubs, shops and parks. Shoppers will find retail bliss in New Town; art aficionados will enjoy the free Scottish National Gallery; and theater hounds will meet their match at August's Edinburgh Festival.

Arrival

Edinburgh has an international airport, Edinburgh Airport (EDI), which is well-connected to major cities in Europe and beyond. From the airport, you can take a taxi, airport shuttle, or the Airlink 100 bus to reach the city center.

Accommodation

Edinburgh offers a wide range of accommodation options to suit different budgets and preferences. The city center, Old Town, and New Town are popular areas to stay due to their proximity to major attractions. Consider booking your accommodation in advance, especially during peak tourist seasons.

Best Months to Visit

The best time to visit Edinburgh is June through August when the average high temperatures rise to a balmy 65 degrees Fahrenheit. But this is also the city's busiest time for tourism, especially in August when festivals fill up the calendar. To avoid spending a small fortune, you'll have to bundle up: winter (November to March) offers the best low-season deals, except during the city's New Year's celebration, Hogmanay. Spring and early fall are the sweet spots – relatively mild weather and thin crowds pair with the chance to find hotel and airfare deals.

Weather in Edinburgh

The weather in Edinburgh can be quite changeable throughout the year, influenced by its maritime climate. Here's a general overview of the weather in Edinburgh:

Spring (March to May)

Spring in Edinburgh is often cool and variable. Daytime temperatures range from around 8°C (46°F) to 14°C (57°F), with occasional rain showers. It's advisable to carry a light jacket and layers for fluctuating temperatures.

Summer (June to August)

Edinburgh experiences mild summers with temperatures ranging from 15°C (59°F) to 20°C (68°F). However, it can occasionally reach higher temperatures. The city sees longer daylight hours, making it a great time to explore. It's recommended to have a mix of light clothing and a sweater or light jacket for cooler evenings.

Autumn (September to November)

Autumn brings cooler temperatures and an increase in rainfall. Daytime temperatures range from 11°C (52°F) to 16°C (61°F), gradually dropping as the season progresses. It's advisable to carry a waterproof jacket and layers to stay comfortable.

Winter (December to February)

Winters in Edinburgh are cold, with temperatures ranging from 2°C (36°F) to 7°C (45°F). Snowfall is not uncommon, especially in the surrounding areas. It's essential to dress warmly with a heavy coat, hat, scarf, and gloves.

How to Save Money in Edinburgh

Saving money in Edinburgh, like in any other city, requires careful planning and smart financial choices. Here are some tips to help you save money while living in Edinburgh:

- Consider sharing a flat or renting a room instead of having your own place to reduce housing costs. Look for accommodation options in less expensive areas outside the city center.

- Be conscious of your energy usage to keep utility bills low. Turn off lights and appliances when not in use, use energy-efficient light bulbs, and set your thermostat to an optimal temperature.

- Utilize public transportation, such as buses and trains, instead of relying on private cars or taxis. Edinburgh has an extensive and well-connected public transport network. Consider purchasing a monthly or yearly pass for further savings.

- While Edinburgh has many tempting restaurants and cafes, dining out frequently can strain your budget. Limit eating out to special occasions and opt for cooking meals at home. Buying groceries and cooking your own food is generally more cost-effective.

- Take advantage of free or low-cost entertainment options available in the city. Visit museums and galleries on their free entry days, explore parks, and participate in community events. Keep an eye on local event listings for free concerts, festivals, and exhibitions.

- Look for discounts, sales, and second-hand options when shopping for clothing, electronics, and household items.

Charity shops and online platforms like Gumtree and eBay can offer affordable alternatives to brand new items.

- Compare prices at different grocery stores to find the best deals. Consider purchasing generic brands and planning your meals in advance to reduce food waste. Shopping with a grocery list can help you avoid impulsive purchases.

- Instead of paying for expensive gym memberships or fitness classes, consider outdoor activities like jogging, cycling, or joining local sports clubs. Edinburgh has numerous parks, hills, and cycle paths that provide great opportunities for exercise.

- Most of Edinburgh's biggest attractions are within a 2-mile radius of one another, so hopping on a bus or tram is unnecessary most of the time.

- Visit in the winter An influx of visitors come to Edinburgh during the summer for festival season. The colder months see fewer visitors and lower room rates.

- Veer off the beaten track Stray from the touristy Royal Mile and Princes Street and you'll likely find better shopping and dining options for a fraction of the price.

What to Eat

Scotland is known for haggis, which – if you really want to know – is sheep's heart, liver and lungs minced together with onions, oatmeal and some seasoning. It's usually served with neeps and tatties, or mashed turnips and potatoes. But note that Edinburgh also offers an array of international cuisine as well, from Thai to Italian. Edinburgh's pubs offer traditionally British cuisine and other comfort food items, including fish and chips and hamburgers, which are also reasonably priced. But if you're willing to take on the haggis challenge, pop on over to Greyfriars Bobby's Bar, the pub located in front of the Greyfriars Bobby memorial, which honors the dog who guarded his deceased master's grave for more than a decade, or Arcade Haggis & Whisky House.

Not keen on trying haggis? Not to worry, Scotland has plenty of other food offerings. One traveler favorite is Makars Gourmet Mash Bar Company, which dishes up hearty favorites like sausages, lamb shank and vegetarian haggis atop mashed potatoes. For a small snack, pop by Pickles. It serves charcuterie boards along with pate, wine and other beverages. For a special occasion, visit Aizle for its delicious seasonal fare.

Many of Edinburgh's restaurants are clustered around Old Town's Royal Mile and New Town's Princes Street. Thanks to its location right by the water, the northern village of Leith is the place to go for fresh seafood. South Edinburgh, or anywhere outside of the city center, also has a variety of cheaper cafes and restaurants for budget-minded travelers. If you want a little help navigating the Edinburgh dining scene, consider signing up for a food tour led by a local.

Safety

Edinburgh is a safe city. It's generally safe to walk around at night, but make sure to know where you're going. Parts of the city, especially Old Town, are filled with winding alleys, closes and wynds, making it easy to get lost at night. Exercise caution for pickpockets in tourist areas, but keep in mind that Edinburgh's low crime rate make pickpockets uncommon in comparison to other big European cities.

Getting Around Edinburgh

The best way to get around Edinburgh is by foot. This hilly city may have you a little out of breath at certain points, but it's still small enough that walking makes the most sense. When you grow tired or want to explore out-of-the-way areas, the city's efficient bus can cart you the rest of the way. A bus – Airlink Shuttle, to be exact – can also bring you from Edinburgh Airport (EDI) into the city center in about the same time as a cab, but for fewer pounds. Once there, you can hop on the city's tram system or explore the city via bus or black cabs, which can be found on high streets (main thoroughfares) and other points of interests throughout town.

Entry & Exit Requirements

A valid travel document is required for United States citizens traveling outside the mainland by air or sea, as well as for U.S. citizens trying to re-enter the country. A United States passport is the preferred form of documentation, and children must have them, too. Note that U.S. citizens do not need a visa unless they plan on staying longer than six months. Visit the U.S. State Department's website for the latest information on the U.K.'s foreign exit and entry requirements.

Travel Costs

Hostel prices:

- 4-8 bed dorm: 16-22 GBP per night

- 10+ bed dorm: 12-14 GBP per night

- Private double room: 50-75 GBP per night

- Budget hotel prices: 50-65 GBP per night

Airbnb:

- Private room: 30 GBP per night

- Entire home/apartment: Starting at 55 GBP per night

Camping:

- Basic plot for tent: 17 GBP per night

- Paid overnight parking, free overnight parking, and campgrounds for car/campervan (using the "park4night" app)

Food:

- Basic meal (Scottish breakfast or haggis): 10-12 GBP

- Pub food (fish and chips, burger): 15-25 GBP

- Three-course meal at a mid-range restaurant: Starting around 30 GBP

- Pint of beer: 4 GBP

- Glass of wine: 5.50 GBP

- Latte or cappuccino: 2.70 GBP

- Classic fish and chips (takeaway): Around 6 GBP

- Chinese takeout: 8-10 GBP

- Basic fast food combo meal: Around 6 GBP

- Street food (food truck): 6-8 GBP

- The Mosque Kitchen (affordable restaurant): 6-8 GBP for an excellent meal

Groceries:

- Weekly groceries: 40-60 GBP (basic staples like pasta, rice, seasonal produce, and some meat)

- Affordable supermarkets: Aldi, Lidl, Asda, and Tesco

Money-Saving Tips

Like the rest of the UK, Edinburgh can be expensive. Fortunately, there are lots of ways to lower your costs and save money here. Here are some quick tips to help you save money in Edinburgh:

Get the Edinburgh City Pass

For 45 GBP, you'll have access to 22 attractions and free transportation to/from the airport. There are also two-day and three-day passes available.

Eat in pubs

Pubs often offer great food at a fraction of the price compared to sit-down restaurants.

Take advantage of lunch deals

Many cafes, bakeries, and chains offer affordable lunch deals ranging from 3-5 GBP.

Use discount apps for food

Use apps like "Too Good to Go" to find severely discounted meals, groceries, and baked goods at the end of the day. For discounted takeout, try the app "Secret Takeaways" to support local restaurants and avoid delivery app fees.

Visit free museums

Scotland's public museums, such as The National Museum of Scotland and the Scottish National Gallery, offer free entry. Explore these attractions without spending money.

Avoid city center prices

Eating and shopping in the city center can be more expensive. Look for good restaurants and shops outside of the center for better prices and unique experiences.

Consider Couchsurfing

Stay with a local through Couchsurfing to save on accommodation costs and gain insights from knowledgeable locals.

Join a free walking tour

Take advantage of free walking tours to learn about the history, architecture, and people of Scotland. These tours are usually a couple of hours long and provide a great introduction to the city.

Cook your own meals

Save money by cooking some of your meals instead of eating out. While it may not be as fancy, it will be cost-effective.

Use discount websites

Check websites like Groupon, Wowcher, and Living Social for deals on accommodation, attractions, and dining options.

Bring a reusable water bottle

Tap water in Scotland is safe to drink, so bring a reusable water bottle to save money and reduce plastic waste. Consider using a brand like LifeStraw, which offers bottles with built-in filters for clean and safe water.

Currency

The official currency is the pound sterling. Since the pound to U.S. dollar exchange rate fluctuates, be sure to check what the current exchange rate is before you go. Major credit cards are accepted at most restaurants and shops. Much like the rest of the U.K. and Europe, tipping is not required. However, if you feel so inclined and your service was exceptional, a 10% tip will be more than enough.

TOP THINGS TO DO AND SEE

See the Edinburgh Castle

T he most famous tourist attraction and at the top of the 'Things to do in Edinburgh' list is the castle located on Castle Rock. Edinburgh Castle was built on volcanic soil and has served as a royal palace and garrison castle for centuries. Today, the castle houses a number of museums, such as the National War Museum. You can also see the Scottish crown jewels in the castle. Visit famous rooms such as the Great Hall and St Margaret's Chapel and learn about the Scottish monarchs and garrisons who have lived here for years. More info 'Edinburgh Castle'.

Old Town & The Royal Mile

Old Town is the district of the Scottish capital, where most of Edinburgh's tourist attractions can be found. The Royal Mile is the main street of this Edinburgh area and consists of the smaller streets: Castlehill, Cannongate, Lawnmarket and High Street. The street runs from Castle Rock, on which Edinburgh Castle is located, to Holyrood Palace. On the Royal Mile you will find attractions such as St. Giles Cathedral, The Scotch Whiskey Experience and the World of Illusions. More info for sightseeing in 'Old Town'.

Visit Edinburgh's Calton Hill

The volcanic mountain of Calton Hill is hundred meters above sea level high and gives you a beautiful view over Edinburgh and The Firth of Forth. The Edinburgh's Calton Hill is home to a number of well-known Scottish monuments constructed in a classical style, making the hill known as the 'Athens of the North'. You will find, for example, the Nelson Monument, Dugald Stewart Monument and the National Monument.

Palace of Holyroodhouse

A monastery was founded by King David I in the twelfth century at the lower part of the Royal Mile, which was soon expanded to become the main residence of the Scottish monarchs. Holyroodhouse was always the residence of the British Queen when she was in Scotland on state affairs. Holyrood Palace contains a number of highlights of the city, such as the Great Gallery, the Queen Gallery and the Palace Gardens.

Royal Yacht Britannia & Leith

For 44 years the ship was the official means of transportation for the British Royal Family by sea: The Royal Yacht Britannia. Today you can visit the yacht in Edinburgh's harbor town of Leith. Tour the royal family's five-deck yacht with an audio guide and learn about the state apartments and crew cabins. The Royal Yacht Britannia was best known for the large state banquets that were organized on deck.

Scotch Whisky Experience

At The Scotch Whiskey Heritage Center you can participate in the Scotch Whiskey Experience. The Experience is part museum, highlighting whiskey, and part an interactive experience, where you will learn more about whiskey distilling through a ride in a whiskey barrel. You really get to know the Scotch whiskey through tasting. At the end of the tour you will enter the tasting room where you can view the largest collection of Scotch whiskeys and try one or more whiskeys depending on your ticket (more info).

Day trips from Edinburgh (Scotland)

Edinburgh's central position makes it easy to make day trips to places of interest in the vicinity of the Scottish capital. You can take boat trips on the Firth of Forth. You can visit the Scottish Highlands with the sharp mountain peaks and famous lakes, such as Loch Ness. Or visit the coastline of Scotland with all kinds of fishing villages, such as St. Andrews. In this article the 13 best day trips in Scotland.

Tip: Are you in Edinburgh for more than two days? Then be sure to book this interesting tour to visit Loch Ness, Glencoe and the Scottish Highlands in one day from Edinburgh. With this day trip you will visit more of Scotland with a very enthusiastic guide and see many tourist attractions of Scotland in 1 day.

Underground Vaults

The infamous South Bridge Vaults are formed in the arches of the South Bridge. They are actually nineteen small rooms, where taverns, workshops and storerooms were located for the first thirty years after the bridge opened in 1788. After this, the Vaults were mainly used as living quarters for vagrants and criminals. Today the northern Underground Vaults are open to the public ghost tours (more info about these tours). The Southern Vaults only host private events, weddings, dinners and parties.

Visit Greyfriars Kirkyard & Greyfriars Bobby

The cemetery of Greyfriars Kirkyard owes its fame to the legend of Greyfriar Bobby, the faithful Sky Terrier who continued to guard his owner's grave until his death. At the entrance of the cemetery, Bobby's tombstone can be seen on the spot where his supposed burial place can be found. The grave of owner John Gray is thirty meters north of the entrance. Greyfriars is also used as a filming location for Harry Potter and the Goblet of Fire. More info for visiting the cemetery and the legend of 'Greyfriars'.

Hiking at Arthur's Seat

Arthur's Seat is the main hill, much of which make up Holyrood Park. At the top of the hill, which rises 251 meters above sea level, enjoy stunning views of Edinburgh and the surrounding area. The 360-degree view is more than worth the steep climb of about an hour. At the top you can also see the large compass and the remains of a hill fort. More info about how to visit 'Arthur's Seat Edinburgh'.

Edinburgh sightseeing by bike

With a rich history, numerous beautiful landmarks and the green surroundings around Arthur's Seat, Edinburgh is the ideal city to discover by bicycle, especially since several highlights and tourist attractions are not within short walking distance of each other. Book this Edinburgh bike tour and go along important Edinburgh sights accompanied by an enthusiastic guide and listen to beautiful stories and anecdotes about the Scottish capital (more info and booking of bike tours).

Sights in Edinburgh 'New Town'

Although not as beautiful as the historic Old Town, the New Town district also offers a number of interesting attractions. Visit for example: Georgian House, Princess Street, George Street, Charlotte Square, Circus Lane and St. Mary's Cathedral. New Town Edinburgh is less historic than the Old Town district, but still beautiful. Circus Lane, for example, is a fairytale scene to see, while Charlotte Square is a beautiful park with an imposing statue.

Monument van Sir Walter Scott

In honor of the acclaimed Scottish author Sir Walter Scott, best known for the historical novel Ivanhoe, the Scott Monument was erected in the Princess Street Gardens. With 61 meters high, it is the second largest monument to a writer. On top of the spire you can see Scott with his dog after a day of writing. On the rest of the monument you can see dozens of other authors.

Dean Village & Water of Leith Walkway

In the Stockbridge district is Dean Village, which was an independent village in the shadow of Edinburgh until the nineteenth century. The village is around The Water of Leith, the main river that flows in Edinburgh. Dean Village was best known for its many mills, which were used to grind grain. The historic houses contain beautiful details and are surrounded by greenery. You can walk along the river via a public walking route. More info to visit 'Dean Village'.

Harry Potter Tour

In addition to London, Edinburgh is also a city where many locations from the Harry Potter books and films occur. Special Harry Potter tours have been set up in Edinburgh for the Potterheads. In Edinburgh town, for example, visit Riddle's cemetery or the cafe where Rowling wrote her first books. Or book a tour outside the city to the Scottish Highlands, where you can ride the Hogwarts Express and visit sites such as the Glenfinnan Viaduct. More info 'Harry Potter Tours'.

Royal Botanic Garden

The Edinburgh Botanic Gardens are definitely a must see. You have free access, with the exception of the ten greenhouses. The botanical garden is part a scientific institution as well as a tourist attraction. The Royal Botanic Garden is 70 hectares in size and contains more than 100,000 different plants in different areas, such as the Rock Garden and the Woodland Garden. From the botanical garden you also have a beautiful view over the skyline of Edinburgh city.

Festival Month August

The month of August is by far the busiest month in Edinburgh. During this month it is definitely high season in the capital because of two appealing festivals. Edinburgh Castle will host the Royal Military Tattoo for several weeks, featuring the impressive displays of the military tattoos. The other three-week event is Edinburgh Fringe, which ranks among the world's largest arts festivals.

Camera Obscura & World of Illusions

One of Edinburgh's renowned attractions is the Camera Obscura and World of Illusions, situated in the former city observatory. At the museum's top floor, visitors can marvel at the Camera Obscura, which offers a breathtaking view of the city. The World of Illusions, on the other hand, is a captivating interactive museum that boasts over a hundred engaging exhibits. From plasma spheres to the Shadow Wall, there are plenty of fascinating experiences to explore. Visitors can delve into the realm of holograms and lifelike 3D displays or venture through the renowned Vortex tunnel.

Edinburgh is home to numerous other museums, and many of them offer free admission. Within the Castle Rock, you'll discover the National War Museum and the Regimental Museum, where you can delve into Scotland's military history. For a comprehensive understanding of Scotland's rich heritage, the National Museum of Scotland is the ideal destination. If optical illusions pique your interest, the World of Illusions provides an interactive and educational exploration of these captivating phenomena. Art enthusiasts can indulge in the artistic offerings of museums such as Jupiter Artland and the Scottish National Gallery. This article presents an overview of 14 museums in Edinburgh, ensuring there's something for everyone to enjoy.

EXPLORING OLD TOWN

xploring Old Town in Edinburgh is a must-do for any visitor. EHere are some recommendations and tips for making the
most of your time in this historic part of the city:

Royal Mile

Start your exploration on the Royal Mile, the main street that runs through Old Town. This iconic street is lined with shops, restaurants, and historic sites. Take your time to wander and soak in the atmosphere.

Edinburgh Castle

Perched atop Castle Rock, Edinburgh Castle is a prominent landmark in Old Town. Explore the castle's various buildings, including the Crown Jewels exhibition, the Great Hall, and St. Margaret's Chapel. The panoramic views of the city from the castle are breathtaking.

St. Giles' Cathedral

Located on the Royal Mile, St. Giles' Cathedral is an impressive medieval church with stunning architecture. Step inside to admire its beautiful stained glass windows and intricate stonework.

The Real Mary King's Close

The Real Mary King's Close is a captivating and unique attraction that allows visitors to explore the hidden underground streets of Old Town in Edinburgh, Scotland. Stepping into this immersive tour is like stepping back in time, as it offers a fascinating glimpse into the city's rich history and the lives of its inhabitants.

The term "close" refers to narrow alleyways or streets that were once bustling with activity and home to vibrant communities. Over time, as the city expanded and modernized, these closes were gradually buried and forgotten, eventually becoming hidden beneath the bustling streets of Edinburgh. The Real Mary King's Close provides a rare opportunity to wander through these forgotten passageways and gain a deeper understanding of the city's past.

Named after Mary King, a prominent figure in the 17th century, this close was once a bustling thoroughfare lined with houses and businesses. The close became buried during the development of the Royal Exchange and subsequent construction projects, preserving its historical significance beneath the modern city.

During the tour, knowledgeable guides lead visitors through the winding labyrinth of underground streets, sharing captivating stories and anecdotes about the people who lived and worked there centuries ago. These tales provide a window into the daily lives, struggles, and triumphs of the past inhabitants, showcasing the social and cultural history of Edinburgh.

As you make your way through the close, you'll witness the well-preserved remnants of these long-lost streets, including reconstructed period rooms that offer a glimpse into the living conditions of the time. The meticulous attention to detail and historical accuracy in the reconstruction transports visitors to a bygone era, evoking a sense of awe and wonder.

The Real Mary King's Close tour not only explores the domestic aspects of life but also delves into the darker side of Edinburgh's history. Stories of disease, poverty, and the occasional ghostly encounter are shared, creating a sense of mystery and intrigue. The atmosphere is further enhanced by the dimly lit underground setting, allowing visitors to truly immerse themselves in the experience.

This attraction appeals to history enthusiasts, curious travelers, and those with a fascination for the supernatural. It offers a unique and memorable experience that educates and entertains in equal measure. The Real Mary King's Close invites visitors to connect with the past, igniting their imagination and leaving a lasting impression of Edinburgh's rich cultural heritage.

Greyfriars Kirkyard

Greyfriars Kirkyard, located in the heart of Edinburgh, is a historic graveyard that holds a unique allure for visitors. With its atmospheric ambiance and fascinating connections to famous literary figures, it offers a captivating journey through history and literature.

One of the most renowned tales associated with Greyfriars Kirkyard is that of Greyfriars Bobby, a loyal Skye Terrier. According to the legend, Bobby faithfully guarded his owner's grave in the cemetery for 14 years. Bobby's story of devotion and loyalty captured the hearts of locals and eventually gained international fame. Today, a statue of Greyfriars Bobby stands near the entrance of the graveyard, serving as a lasting tribute to his remarkable tale.

In addition to Greyfriars Bobby, Greyfriars Kirkyard has strong connections to another literary phenomenon: J.K. Rowling and her famous Harry Potter series. Rowling resided in Edinburgh while writing the early books of the series and found inspiration in the city's rich history and landmarks, including Greyfriars Kirkyard.

Several gravestones in the cemetery bear names that resemble those of Harry Potter characters. For instance, the tombstone of Thomas Riddell inspired the name of the infamous Lord Voldemort's alter ego, Tom Riddle. Rowling also drew inspiration from other names found within the kirkyard, such as William McGonagall, which served as the basis for the beloved Hogwarts professor, Minerva McGonagall.

Exploring Greyfriars Kirkyard provides an opportunity to stroll among weathered tombstones and soak in the quiet beauty of the surroundings. The graveyard exudes a sense of history and reverence, with its ancient architecture, moss-covered monuments, and age-worn epitaphs. Walking through its paths, visitors can't help but feel a connection to the past and a deep appreciation for the lives and stories that have shaped the city.

Beyond its literary and historical significance, Greyfriars Kirkyard also offers an insight into Edinburgh's rich religious heritage. The graveyard is adjacent to the Greyfriars Kirk, a church dating back to the 17th century. The church's striking architecture and serene interior make it a place of reflection and contemplation.

Moreover, Greyfriars Kirkyard is not only a place frozen in time but also a living testament to the city's enduring spirit. It remains an active burial ground, with new interments taking place alongside the centuries-old graves. This juxtaposition of past and present creates a palpable sense of continuity and reminds visitors of the ongoing connection between the people of Edinburgh and their history.

The National Museum of Scotland

Situated in a stunning Victorian building, the museum houses a vast collection of artifacts showcasing Scotland's history, culture, and natural heritage.

Victoria Street

Don't miss Victoria Street, a picturesque curved street lined with colorful buildings housing unique shops and boutiques. It's a great place to find souvenirs and enjoy the charming atmosphere.

Dynamic Earth

The interactive museum you're referring to is a captivating and educational destination that takes visitors on an immersive journey through the Earth's history, climate, and natural phenomena. It offers a unique and engaging experience that appeals to people of all ages, providing a wealth of knowledge and understanding about our planet and its remarkable story.

As you step into the museum, you are immediately greeted by interactive exhibits that bring the Earth's history to life. From the formation of the planet to the evolution of life, each section offers a captivating exploration of geological and biological processes. Through engaging displays, realistic reconstructions, and multimedia presentations, visitors can witness the birth of continents, the shifting of tectonic plates, and the emergence of diverse ecosystems.

One of the highlights of the museum is its focus on climate change and its impact on our planet. Through interactive simulations, visitors can understand the causes and consequences of global warming, exploring the interconnectedness of human activities and the environment. They can also learn about the importance of sustainability and discover practical ways to mitigate the effects of climate change in their daily lives.

Natural phenomena are another key aspect of the museum's offerings. Visitors can experience simulated earthquakes, volcanic eruptions, and severe weather events in a safe and controlled environment. These immersive displays provide a firsthand understanding of the power and unpredictability of nature, fostering a sense of awe and respect for the Earth's forces.

To enhance the learning experience, the museum employs state-of-the-art technology such as virtual reality, augmented reality, and interactive touch screens. These tools allow visitors to engage with the exhibits in a hands-on manner, deepening their understanding and making the educational journey both enjoyable and memorable.

The museum also caters to different learning styles and age groups. It offers educational programs and workshops designed specifically for school groups, providing a curriculum-aligned experience that complements classroom learning. Additionally, guided tours and knowledgeable staff are available to answer questions and provide further insights into the exhibits.

Beyond its educational value, the museum aims to inspire visitors to become stewards of the planet. By fostering an appreciation for the Earth's natural wonders and the importance of conservation, it encourages individuals to make sustainable choices and contribute to the preservation of our environment.

Calton Hill

While not technically part of Old Town, Calton Hill offers fantastic views of the city and is just a short walk away. Climb to the top and enjoy panoramic vistas, including the iconic view of the city with the National Monument and the Nelson Monument.

Arthur's Seat

Nestled within Holyrood Park in Edinburgh, Scotland, Arthur's Seat stands as an ancient volcano, offering both a remarkable geological landmark and a beloved recreational area for locals and visitors alike. This iconic natural formation provides a wonderful opportunity for hiking, exploration, and the chance to immerse oneself in breathtaking panoramic views of the city.

Arthur's Seat holds a significant place in Edinburgh's history and mythology. Its name is thought to be derived from the legendary King Arthur, adding an air of enchantment to the site. The volcano itself has been extinct for millions of years, leaving behind a rugged and distinctive landscape that captivates the imagination.

The ascent to Arthur's Seat is a popular activity, drawing hikers, nature enthusiasts, and those seeking tranquility in the midst of a bustling city. A well-maintained network of trails weaves its way up the hill, catering to various fitness levels and providing options for leisurely walks or more challenging hikes. As you ascend, the surrounding flora and fauna create a sense of serenity, with wildflowers, grassy meadows, and occasional wildlife sightings adding to the charm.

Reaching the summit of Arthur's Seat is a rewarding experience. From the top, visitors are greeted with awe-inspiring vistas that stretch across the city of Edinburgh, its historic landmarks, and the surrounding natural beauty. The panoramic views encompass the magnificent Edinburgh Castle, the striking architecture of the Old Town, the dramatic coastline, and even the distant peaks of the Scottish Highlands on clear days. This vantage point offers a unique perspective on the city, allowing visitors to appreciate its rich history and stunning landscapes.

Beyond its scenic allure, Arthur's Seat holds a special place in the hearts of locals. It serves as a gathering place for community events, picnics, and outdoor activities. Whether it's a jog around the trails, a yoga session with a view, or a leisurely afternoon spent reading a book on one of the grassy slopes, the park provides a sense of escape from the urban bustle, inviting visitors to connect with nature and find solace in its peaceful surroundings.

Moreover, the geological and ecological significance of Arthur's Seat cannot be overlooked. It serves as a designated Site of Special Scientific Interest, attracting geologists and researchers interested in its unique rock formations and the diverse plant and animal life that call it home. The park's conservation efforts help preserve the natural ecosystem and ensure its accessibility for generations to come.

DISCOVERING NEW TOWN

iscovering New Town in Edinburgh offers a contrasting Dexperience to Old Town. Here are some suggestions for exploring this elegant and Georgian part of the city:

Princes Street

Begin your exploration on Princes Street, the main thoroughfare in New Town. This bustling street is lined with shops, department stores, and beautiful gardens. Enjoy the stunning views of the Edinburgh Castle from here.

Princes Street Gardens

Nestled between Edinburgh's Old Town and New Town, the Princes Street Gardens offer a serene and picturesque haven amidst the vibrant cityscape. Spanning a vast area, these gardens provide a tranquil escape where visitors can immerse themselves in natural beauty, admire vibrant floral displays, meander along winding paths, and bask in the peaceful ambiance of the well-maintained lawns.

The gardens owe their name to the fact that they lie beneath the iconic Princes Street, one of Edinburgh's main thoroughfares. This location grants visitors breathtaking views of the Edinburgh Castle towering atop Castle Rock, forming a majestic backdrop to the gardens' tranquil atmosphere.

As you enter the Princes Street Gardens, you'll be greeted by a feast for the senses. The meticulously tended flower beds showcase a riot of colors, with seasonal blooms adding vibrancy to the landscape. From daffodils and tulips in the spring to roses and dahlias in the summer, the gardens offer a visually captivating display throughout the year.

The gardens boast an extensive network of paths, allowing visitors to explore at their own pace. Take a leisurely stroll along the tree-lined walkways, meandering past manicured hedges and ornamental shrubs. As you wander, you'll encounter various sculptures and monuments that pay homage to significant figures from Scotland's history, adding cultural interest to your journey.

For those seeking a moment of relaxation, the lush lawns provide an inviting space to unwind. Find a comfortable spot to sit, spread out a picnic blanket, and soak up the tranquil atmosphere. Whether you're enjoying a quiet moment alone, sharing laughter and conversation with friends, or watching families play, the Princes Street Gardens offer an idyllic setting for peaceful contemplation and rejuvenation.

The gardens also host a variety of events and festivals throughout the year, adding an extra touch of liveliness to the surroundings. From summer concerts and outdoor theater performances to festive markets during the holiday season, there's often something happening that enhances the already enchanting ambiance.

Moreover, the location of the Princes Street Gardens makes it a perfect starting point for exploring other nearby attractions. Just a stone's throw away is the historic Royal Mile, leading to the iconic Edinburgh Castle. The gardens also serve as a gateway to the bustling shops, restaurants, and cultural landmarks of the New Town, making it a convenient and pleasant starting point for further exploration of the city.

Georgian Architecture

New Town is renowned for its neoclassical Georgian architecture. As you wander the streets, marvel at the elegant townhouses, grand squares, and intricate details on the buildings. Some notable streets to explore include George Street, Charlotte Square, and Moray Place.

Scott Monument

Standing tall in Princes Street Gardens is the Scott Monument, dedicated to Scottish writer Sir Walter Scott. Climb the narrow spiral staircase inside for panoramic views of the city from the top.

National Portrait Gallery

Visit the National Portrait Gallery on Queen Street, which houses a vast collection of portraits depicting influential Scottish figures throughout history. Explore the gallery's exhibitions and admire the impressive Victorian architecture.

St. Andrew Square

Head to St. Andrew Square, one of the largest and most prestigious squares in Edinburgh. Enjoy the green space, relax on the benches, and visit the Melville Monument, a statue honoring Henry Dundas, Viscount Melville.

Stockbridge

Take a short walk north of New Town to Stockbridge, a charming neighborhood with a village-like atmosphere. Explore the quaint streets lined with independent shops, boutiques, cafes, and the vibrant Stockbridge Market (held on Sundays).

Dean Village

Situated just a short walk west of Edinburgh's New Town, Dean Village is a hidden gem that transports visitors to a bygone era. This picturesque area is renowned for its charming cottages, narrow streets, and the tranquil Water of Leith that meanders through its heart. A visit to Dean Village offers a serene and idyllic escape from the hustle and bustle of the city.

As you enter Dean Village, you'll be greeted by a scene straight out of a postcard. The quaint cottages, with their well-preserved architecture, line the cobblestone streets, creating an enchanting atmosphere reminiscent of a storybook village. Many of these historic buildings were once home to mill workers during Edinburgh's industrial past, adding a touch of history to the area's charm.

The focal point of Dean Village is the Water of Leith, a scenic river that flows gently through the heart of the neighborhood. Follow the riverside path, and you'll find yourself immersed in a serene natural setting. The tranquil sound of flowing water, combined with the lush greenery that lines the riverbanks, creates a soothing ambiance that invites visitors to unwind and enjoy the peaceful surroundings.

A leisurely walk along the riverside path offers stunning vistas at every turn. The tree-lined banks, with their vibrant foliage, provide a picturesque backdrop against the rushing water. Bridges, both old and new, span the river, offering charming viewpoints and photo opportunities.

As you explore Dean Village, keep an eye out for the remnants of its industrial past. You may come across the occasional millstone or old mill building, serving as a reminder of the area's historical significance. The contrast between the natural beauty and the traces of industrial heritage adds depth to the experience, giving you a glimpse into the evolution of the village over time.

Dean Village is not only a place of tranquility but also a starting point for further exploration. The Water of Leith Walkway, which stretches for 12 miles along the river, provides an opportunity for longer walks or cycling adventures. Following this scenic route allows you to discover more of Edinburgh's natural beauty, passing through charming neighborhoods, parks, and even the impressive Dean Bridge.

National Galleries of Scotland

Comprising several galleries, including the Scottish National Gallery, the Scottish National Portrait Gallery, and the Scottish National Gallery of Modern Art, these institutions showcase a rich collection of art from various periods.

The Scottish National Gallery

Located on the Mound, between Old Town and New Town, The Scottish National Gallery houses an extensive collection of fine art, including works by Scottish and international artists. Explore the galleries and appreciate the masterpieces on display.

Charlotte Square Gardens

To conclude your exploration of Edinburgh, a visit to Charlotte Square Gardens is a fitting choice. Situated in the heart of the New Town, this elegant garden square showcases the architectural grandeur and cultural vibrancy of the city. Designed by renowned architect Robert Adam in the late 18th century, Charlotte Square Gardens is a captivating space surrounded by beautifully preserved Georgian townhouses.

As you step into the gardens, you'll be greeted by a serene and meticulously manicured oasis. The lush green lawns, vibrant flowerbeds, and well-maintained paths create a tranquil setting that invites visitors to relax and soak in the elegant atmosphere. The symmetrical layout of the square, a hallmark of Georgian design, lends a sense of order and harmony to the space.

One of the notable features of Charlotte Square Gardens is the beautiful central garden, which serves as a focal point for the square. This well-designed green space is adorned with ornamental trees, shrubs, and flowers, creating a captivating display throughout the seasons. It provides an ideal spot for a leisurely stroll or a moment of contemplation.

Charlotte Square Gardens is not only a haven of natural beauty but also a hub for literary enthusiasts. Each year, during the summer months, the gardens come alive with the Edinburgh International Book Festival. This renowned event attracts authors, readers, and literary enthusiasts from around the world. The festival offers a vibrant program of talks, readings, and book signings, making it an exciting destination for literature lovers.

Surrounding the gardens are the elegant Georgian townhouses that contribute to the square's architectural splendor. These magnificent buildings, with their distinctive facades, stand as a testament to the city's rich heritage. Many of these townhouses have been meticulously preserved and now serve as prestigious residences, commercial spaces, or headquarters for cultural organizations.

Charlotte Square Gardens also enjoys a central location, making it a convenient starting point for further exploration. The square is within walking distance of other notable attractions, including the iconic Princes Street, the historic Royal Mile, and the majestic Edinburgh Castle. Embarking on a stroll from Charlotte Square Gardens allows you to seamlessly transition from the tranquility of the gardens to the vibrant energy of the surrounding areas.

EDINBURGH FESTIVALS

dinburgh is famous for its vibrant festival scene, attracting Evisitors from all over the world. Here are some of the major
festivals held in Edinburgh:

Edinburgh International Festival

Running concurrently with the Fringe, the Edinburgh International Festival showcases world-class performing arts, including theater, opera, music, and dance. It focuses on high-quality productions from renowned artists and companies.

Edinburgh International Book Festival

Held in August, the Edinburgh International Book Festival brings together writers, poets, and literary enthusiasts from around the globe. It features author talks, book signings, panel discussions, and workshops, covering a wide range of literary genres and topics.

Edinburgh International Film Festival

As the longest-running film festival in the world, the Edinburgh International Film Festival celebrates international cinema. It showcases a diverse range of feature films, documentaries, shorts, and experimental works.

Edinburgh Festival Fringe

The Edinburgh Festival Fringe, the largest arts festival in the world, is a vibrant celebration of creativity and performance that takes place annually throughout the month of August in Edinburgh, Scotland. This iconic event attracts artists, performers, and visitors from around the globe, transforming the city into a cultural hub and immersing attendees in a kaleidoscope of artistic experiences.

The festival encompasses a vast array of art forms, including theatre, comedy, dance, music, circus acts, spoken word, and much more. With thousands of shows and performances taking place in various venues across the city, there is something to captivate and inspire every audience member. From internationally acclaimed productions to emerging talent and experimental performances, the Edinburgh Festival Fringe offers a diverse and eclectic program that pushes the boundaries of creativity.

What sets the Fringe apart is its inclusive and open-access nature. Artists from all backgrounds and levels of experience are welcome to participate, enabling a dynamic and diverse lineup. This democratic approach allows emerging artists to showcase their talents alongside established performers, creating a melting pot of creativity and innovation.

The festival not only takes place within traditional theater venues but also spills out onto the streets, parks, and pop-up spaces throughout the city. Street performers and buskers add an additional layer of excitement and entertainment, creating a festive atmosphere that permeates every corner of Edinburgh during the Fringe. The streets come alive with music, comedy skits, acrobatics, and interactive performances, delighting both passersby and dedicated festival-goers.

The Fringe's lively and bustling atmosphere extends beyond the performances themselves. The city becomes a hub of socializing, networking, and artistic exploration. The famous Royal Mile, a bustling thoroughfare in the heart of the city, becomes a vibrant hub of promotion, where performers hand out flyers and entice audiences to their shows. Visitors can also explore pop-up bars, food stalls, and art installations that further enhance the festival experience.

Attending the Edinburgh Festival Fringe is not just about watching performances; it's an immersive and interactive experience. It encourages active participation, dialogue, and discovery. Audiences have the opportunity to engage with artists, share their experiences, and contribute to the lively exchange of ideas and creativity.

Edinburgh International Science Festival

The Edinburgh International Science Festival is an educational and interactive festival that takes place in April. It offers a wide range of events, exhibitions, workshops, and discussions exploring various scientific disciplines and topics.

Edinburgh Jazz & Blues Festival

Every July, Edinburgh becomes a vibrant hub for jazz and blues enthusiasts from around the world as it hosts the highly anticipated Edinburgh Jazz & Blues Festival. This renowned event showcases the best of these genres, featuring an impressive lineup of local and international artists, captivating performances, and a variety of engaging events.

The festival offers a diverse range of concerts that cater to different tastes within the jazz and blues genres. From traditional jazz ensembles to contemporary fusion acts and from classic blues to soulful performances, the program presents an eclectic mix of styles and influences. Attendees can experience the dynamic energy of live performances in various venues throughout the city, from concert halls and theaters to intimate club settings.

In addition to the concerts, the Edinburgh Jazz & Blues Festival fosters a sense of community and participation through jam sessions and workshops. Musicians of all levels and backgrounds are encouraged to join in, creating a platform for collaboration and creative exchange. These jam sessions provide an opportunity for both seasoned musicians and aspiring artists to come together, share their love for jazz and blues, and create music in an informal and spontaneous setting.

The festival also offers workshops and masterclasses led by renowned artists, providing a chance for attendees to enhance their skills, learn from experienced musicians, and deepen their understanding of the genres. These educational components add an enriching dimension to the festival, nurturing talent and fostering a passion for jazz and blues in the next generation of artists.

As the sun sets, the Edinburgh Jazz & Blues Festival keeps the energy alive with club nights that showcase the vibrant nightlife scene. These events offer a more intimate setting where attendees can enjoy performances in cozy venues, dance to the infectious rhythms, and revel in the festive atmosphere.

The festival not only celebrates established artists but also provides a platform for emerging talent. It actively supports local musicians, giving them a chance to showcase their skills alongside international performers, fostering a sense of artistic community and showcasing the rich musical landscape of Edinburgh.

Beyond the performances, the festival contributes to the cultural vibrancy of Edinburgh. It attracts music lovers, visitors, and locals alike, adding an exciting energy to the city's summer calendar. Attendees can explore the historic streets of Edinburgh during the day and immerse themselves in the sounds and rhythms of jazz and blues during the evening, creating an unforgettable fusion of music and cultural experiences.

Edinburgh Festival of The Royal Mile

Celebrating the culture and history of the Royal Mile, this festival features street performances, live music, storytelling, and historical reenactments. It provides a unique opportunity to immerse yourself in the heritage of Edinburgh's iconic street.

Edinburgh Art Festival

Showcasing contemporary and visual arts, the Edinburgh Art Festival presents a wide range of exhibitions, installations, and performances across the city's galleries, museums, and public spaces. It takes place from July to August.

FOOD AND DRINK

hen it comes to food and drink in Edinburgh, you'll find a W wide range of options to suit every taste and budget. Here are some recommendations for experiencing the culinary
scene in the city:

Traditional Edinburgh Cuisine

Sample classic Scottish dishes such as haggis, neeps and tatties (turnips and potatoes), Scotch broth, Cullen skink (smoked haddock soup), and cranachan (a dessert made with raspberries, cream, oats, and whisky). Many traditional Scottish restaurants and pubs in Edinburgh offer these dishes. While Edinburgh shares many traditional Scottish dishes, it also has some regional specialties that are unique to the city. Here are a few traditional Edinburgh dishes you should try during your visit:

Edinburgh Mutton Pie

A classic savory pie made with tender mutton, onions, and spices, encased in a flaky pastry crust. This hearty pie is a traditional Edinburgh delicacy that dates back centuries.

Cullen Skink

While Cullen Skink is a popular Scottish dish, it has a special place in Edinburgh cuisine. This creamy smoked haddock soup, made with potatoes, onions, and milk, is a comforting and flavorsome treat.

Tipsy Laird

Tipsy Laird is a traditional Scottish trifle, and it's often enjoyed in Edinburgh. This indulgent dessert is made with layers of sponge cake, raspberries, custard, and whisky-infused cream.

Edinburgh Gin

Edinburgh has a thriving gin scene, and local distilleries produce a variety of unique and flavorful gins. Try a gin and tonic or sample some creative gin cocktails to experience the city's gin culture.

Dunlop Cheese

Although not exclusive to Edinburgh, Dunlop cheese is a popular Scottish cheese that you can find in the city. It's a semi-hard cheese with a slightly crumbly texture and a mild, nutty flavor.

Clootie Dumpling

Clootie Dumpling is a traditional Scottish dessert that's occasionally found in Edinburgh. It's a steamed pudding made with dried fruit, spices, breadcrumbs, and suet, and it's typically served with a sweet sauce or custard.

Forfar Bridies

While not native to Edinburgh, Forfar Bridies are popular pastries in the city. These savory meat-filled turnovers, typically made with minced beef, onions, and spices, are a tasty snack or lunch option.

Tablet

Tablet is a sweet Scottish confection that resembles fudge. Made with sugar, butter, and condensed milk, this crumbly treat is often enjoyed alongside a cup of tea or as a souvenir to take home.

Pub Grub

Enjoy hearty pub food, which often includes dishes like fish and chips, steak and ale pie, and Scotch eggs. Pubs are great places to experience local atmosphere and enjoy a pint of Scottish ale or whisky. Here are some popular pub grub options to try while in the city:

Fish and Chips

A classic British dish, fish and chips is a must-try in Edinburgh. Enjoy crispy battered fish, usually haddock or cod, served with chunky chips (fries) and accompanied by tartar sauce and mushy peas.

Steak and Ale Pie

Indulge in a comforting steak and ale pie. This savory pie is filled with tender chunks of beef, onions, and a rich ale gravy, topped with a golden pastry crust. It's often served with mashed potatoes or chips.

Scotch Egg

A Scotch egg is a boiled egg wrapped in sausage meat, coated in breadcrumbs, and deep-fried until crispy. It's a popular pub snack or appetizer that pairs well with a pint of beer.

Ploughman's Lunch

A Ploughman's lunch is a classic pub dish featuring a selection of cold meats (such as ham or roast beef), cheese, pickles, chutney, bread, and butter. It's a satisfying and traditional choice for a light meal.

Bangers and Mash

Bangers and mash is a beloved pub staple. It consists of flavorful sausages served with creamy mashed potatoes and often accompanied by onion gravy.

Chicken Tikka Masala

While not traditionally Scottish, chicken tikka masala is a popular dish in British pubs. Tender pieces of chicken are cooked in a creamy and spiced tomato-based sauce, served with rice or naan bread.

Steak

Many pubs in Edinburgh offer delicious steaks cooked to perfection. You can choose from various cuts such as sirloin, ribeye, or fillet, and often have the option to add sides like mushrooms, grilled tomatoes, or onion rings.

Burgers

Pubs in Edinburgh often serve tasty burgers, ranging from classic beef burgers to gourmet creations. These are usually accompanied by fries or coleslaw and offer a satisfying and filling meal.

Pies

Pubs are known for their savory pies, such as chicken and mushroom, steak and kidney, or vegetable pies. These are typically served with sides like mashed potatoes, peas, and gravy.

Scotch Broth

While it's not exclusive to pubs, you may find Scotch broth on the menu. This hearty soup, made with lamb or beef, barley, vegetables, and herbs, is a comforting and traditional option.

Seafood

Being a coastal city, Edinburgh is known for its fresh seafood. Try dishes like smoked salmon, mussels, oysters, and locally caught fish. The seafood restaurants along the shore in Leith are particularly renowned.

Afternoon Tea

Treat yourself to a traditional afternoon tea experience in one of Edinburgh's elegant tea rooms or hotels. Indulge in a selection of finger sandwiches, scones with clotted cream and jam, and an assortment of cakes and pastries, accompanied by a pot of tea.

International Cuisine

Edinburgh boasts a diverse range of international cuisines. You'll find excellent options for Italian, Indian, Chinese, Thai, Japanese, Mexican, and more. Explore neighborhoods like Leith, Bruntsfield, and Stockbridge for a variety of international dining experiences.

Whisky Tastings

Scotland is famous for its whisky, and Edinburgh offers various whisky tasting experiences. Visit whisky bars or specialist shops to sample different single malts or join a guided tasting tour to learn about the production and flavors of Scottish whisky.

Farmers' Markets

Visit one of Edinburgh's farmers' markets to discover locally sourced produce, artisanal products, and tasty treats. The popular markets include the Edinburgh Farmers' Market (Saturdays), Stockbridge Market (Sundays), and the Grassmarket Market (Saturdays). Here are a few notable farmers' markets in Edinburgh:

Edinburgh Farmers' Market

Held every Saturday at Castle Terrace, near the historic Old Town, this market features a range of local farmers, producers, and vendors offering fruits, vegetables, meats, cheeses, baked goods, preserves, and more.

Stockbridge Market

Taking place every Sunday in the charming neighborhood of Stockbridge, this market offers a delightful selection of organic produce, specialty foods, handmade crafts, and street food stalls. It's a great place to explore on a leisurely Sunday morning.

Leith Market

Held on Saturdays at Dock Place in the vibrant district of Leith, this market showcases local food producers, artisans, and street food vendors. Visitors can find everything from fresh produce to handmade crafts and enjoy a lively atmosphere.

Grassmarket Farmers' Market

Located near the historic Grassmarket area, this market operates on Saturdays and offers a range of fresh produce, artisanal foods, locally brewed beers, and unique crafts. It's a fantastic spot to soak up the lively ambiance of the city.

Craft Beer

Edinburgh has a thriving craft beer scene, with numerous breweries and pubs offering a wide selection of locally brewed beers. Explore breweries, taprooms, and beer bars to taste a range of unique and flavorful craft beers.

Gin Distilleries

Gin enthusiasts can explore the gin distilleries in Edinburgh, which offer tours and tastings. Learn about the production process, botanicals, and enjoy a refreshing gin and tonic or cocktail.

Food Festivals

Check if any food festivals or events are taking place during your visit. Edinburgh hosts various food-related events throughout the year, such as the Edinburgh Food Festival, where you can indulge in local and international cuisines.

SHOPPING IN EDINBURGH

Shopping in Edinburgh offers a diverse range of options, from high-end boutiques and department stores to independent shops and unique markets. Here are some popular shopping areas and recommendations for your Edinburgh shopping experience:

Shop at Princes Street

Princes Street is the main shopping street in Edinburgh, offering a mix of high-street stores, popular brands, and department stores. You'll find shops like Primark, Zara, and H&M, as well as department stores like Jenners and Debenhams.

Shop at George Street

Located parallel to Princes Street, George Street is known for its upscale shops, designer boutiques, and luxury brands. Explore stores like Harvey Nichols, Anthropologie, and Jo Malone for a more indulgent shopping experience.

Shop at Grassmarket

Grassmarket is a historic and vibrant area filled with independent shops, boutiques, and vintage stores. Explore the unique shops offering clothing, antiques, books, crafts, and more. Don't miss the

Grassmarket Market on weekends for a variety of artisanal products and local crafts.

Shop at Multrees Walk

Located adjacent to St. Andrew Square, Multrees Walk stands as Edinburgh's premier luxury shopping destination. This stylish pedestrian street is lined with a carefully curated selection of high-end brands, making it a paradise for luxury fashion and accessories shopping.

Multrees Walk is home to some of the world's most renowned luxury brands, each offering a unique and exceptional shopping experience. From fashion powerhouses like Louis Vuitton, Burberry, Gucci, and Mulberry to fine jewelry and watch boutiques such as Rolex and Hamilton & Inches, the street boasts an impressive array of choices for discerning shoppers.

Entering Multrees Walk, you'll immediately notice the chic and sophisticated atmosphere. The street's sleek and modern design, coupled with its well-manicured surroundings, creates an ambiance that perfectly complements the luxurious shopping experience it offers. Impeccable storefronts and elegant window displays showcase the latest fashion trends and coveted pieces, beckoning visitors to explore further.

Inside the boutiques, you'll find an extensive range of designer clothing, accessories, and luxury goods. From exquisite handbags and leather goods to designer clothing, shoes, and accessories, Multrees Walk has something to cater to every discerning taste. The knowledgeable staff in each boutique provide personalized service, ensuring that every shopper receives the attention and guidance they need to find the perfect piece.

Aside from luxury fashion, Multrees Walk also hosts a selection of upscale beauty and lifestyle stores. Perfume aficionados can indulge in the scents of brands such as Jo Malone, Penhaligon's, and Frederic Malle, while beauty enthusiasts can explore high -end cosmetics and skincare products from stores like Space NK and Harvey Nichols.

When you need a break from shopping, Multrees Walk offers a selection of upscale dining options where you can refuel and recharge. From sophisticated cafés serving artisanal coffee to elegant restaurants offering culinary delights, you can enjoy a well-deserved meal or a relaxing cup of tea amidst the refined ambiance of the street.

Multrees Walk's location is also advantageous, as it is just a short walk from other popular attractions and shopping areas in the city center. Visitors can easily explore the neighboring Princes Street, George Street, and the historic Royal Mile, further enriching their Edinburgh shopping experience.

Shop at Victoria Street

Known for its charming and colorful architecture, Victoria Street is lined with boutique shops, independent retailers, and specialty stores. It's a great place to find unique gifts, jewelry, clothing, and Scottish souvenirs.

Shop at Stockbridge

The Stockbridge neighborhood is a hub for independent shops and boutiques. Discover vintage stores, art galleries, bookshops, and artisan food shops. Stockbridge Market, held on Sundays, offers local produce, crafts, and street food.

Shop at Royal Mile

The historic Royal Mile is not just for sightseeing; it's also home to a variety of shops selling tartans, kilts, whisky, souvenirs, and Scottish crafts. Explore the shops along this iconic street to find traditional Scottish products.

Shop at West End

Nestled in the heart of Edinburgh, the West End is a trendy and vibrant neighborhood renowned for its diverse and eclectic shopping scene. This bustling area is a haven for those seeking unique fashion, homeware, vintage clothing, and local designer pieces, offering a delightful mix of independent shops, boutiques, and design stores.

Exploring the West End reveals a treasure trove of distinctive fashion finds. Independent clothing boutiques line the streets, showcasing a curated selection of stylish garments that cater to a range of tastes. Here, you can discover local designer pieces, one-of-a-kind items, and emerging fashion labels that embody the essence of Edinburgh's creative spirit.

The West End is also a haven for those in search of unique homeware and interior design. Quaint shops and design stores offer an array of handpicked treasures, from contemporary furniture to quirky decor pieces that add personality to any home. Whether you're looking for statement furniture, artful ceramics, or delightful textiles, the West End provides a wealth of options to help you curate a space that reflects your individual style.

Vintage enthusiasts will delight in the West End's selection of vintage clothing stores and thrift shops. These charming establishments offer an extensive range of carefully curated vintage pieces, allowing shoppers to uncover hidden gems from bygone eras. From retro fashion finds to classic accessories, exploring these stores is like stepping into a sartorial time capsule.

In addition to fashion and homeware, the West End is a hub for local designers and artisans. Pop into the independent boutiques and concept stores to discover unique handmade jewelry, accessories, and crafts. These locally made treasures often reflect the rich cultural heritage and contemporary creativity of Edinburgh, providing a truly authentic shopping experience.

Beyond its diverse retail offerings, the West End exudes a vibrant and welcoming atmosphere. Its charming streets are lined with inviting cafes, stylish eateries, and cozy pubs, making it an ideal place to take a break and enjoy a cup of coffee or a leisurely meal. You can soak in the local ambiance, mingle with the creative community, and refuel before continuing your shopping adventure.

The West End's central location also allows for easy exploration of other nearby attractions. Within walking distance, you can discover the iconic Edinburgh Castle, the historic Grassmarket, and the bustling Princes Street, adding further variety to your Edinburgh experience.

Shop at Princes Mall and St. James Quarter

Princes Mall, located near Waverley Station, offers a range of shops including fashion, accessories, and beauty. Additionally, the recently opened St. James Quarter is a new shopping destination featuring a mix of high-street and luxury brands, along with dining options.

SOUVENIRS FROM EDINBURGH

hen visiting Edinburgh, you'll find a wide range of unique W and traditional souvenirs to take home as mementos of your trip. Here are some popular souvenirs from Edinburgh:

Tartan Products

Scotland is famous for its tartan patterns. Look for tartan scarves, blankets, ties, and kilts as traditional Scottish souvenirs. You can find them in various colors and patterns, representing different clans or regions.

Whisky

Scotland is renowned for its whisky production. Consider purchasing a bottle of single malt Scotch whisky as a special souvenir. You can find a variety of brands and age ranges to suit different tastes and budgets.

Shortbread

Scottish shortbread is a delicious treat that makes for a tasty souvenir. Look for traditional shortbread biscuits or tins filled with different flavors like plain, chocolate chip, or fruit-infused varieties.

Edinburgh Gin

Gin lovers can bring home a bottle of Edinburgh Gin. This award-winning gin is crafted locally and comes in different flavors, such as raspberry, rhubarb, or classic London dry style. You can also find gin-related accessories like glasses or cocktail recipe books.

Scottish Tartan Woolens

Visit one of the local woolen mills or shops to find a range of Scottish textiles. From blankets and throws to scarves and gloves, these woolen products often feature traditional patterns and are perfect for staying warm or adding a touch of Scottish heritage to your home.

Edinburgh Castle Memorabilia

As a symbol of the city, Edinburgh Castle-related souvenirs are popular. Look for keychains, magnets, postcards, or replicas of the castle itself to bring a piece of its history back with you.

Celtic Jewelry

Scotland has a rich Celtic heritage, and you can find a wide selection of Celtic-inspired jewelry. From intricate knotwork designs to thistle motifs, consider purchasing a piece of jewelry like a pendant, bracelet, or earrings.

Scottish Shortbread

Another sweet treat to bring back home is Scottish shortbread. Look for tins or boxes of this buttery biscuit that is often presented in beautiful packaging, making it a great gift for friends and family.

Highland Cow Souvenirs

The iconic Highland cow, with its shaggy coat and majestic horns, is a symbol of Scotland. If you're looking for Highland cow souvenirs, here are some popular options:

Plush Toys

Look for plush Highland cow toys that capture the charm and cuteness of these animals. They make excellent cuddly souvenirs for both children and adults.

Figurines and Ornaments

Highland cow figurines or ornaments are great for decorating your home or office. They come in various materials such as resin, ceramic, or metal, and can be found in different sizes and poses.

Clothing and Accessories

Show your love for Highland cows by wearing T-shirts, hoodies, or hats featuring their images. You can also find accessories like keychains, pins, or socks with Highland cow designs.

Art Prints and Posters

Adorn your walls with beautiful art prints or posters featuring Highland cows. These pieces of art capture the majestic appearance and rugged beauty of these animals.

Mugs and Kitchenware

Enjoy your cup of tea or coffee in a Highland cow-themed mug. You can also find other kitchenware like coasters, tea towels, or aprons featuring these beloved creatures.

Edinburgh Travel Guide 2024 and Beyond

Calendars and Stationery

Keep track of your schedule with a Highland cow-themed calendar or planner. Additionally, you can find notepads, pens, and other stationery items adorned with Highland cow designs.

Books and Guides

Learn more about Highland cows with books or guides that provide insights into their history, characteristics, and their importance in Scottish culture.

Photography and Artwork

Look for framed photographs or artwork that showcase Highland cows in all their glory. These pieces can add a touch of Scottish charm to any room.

Keychains and Magnets

Highland cow keychains and magnets are small, affordable souvenirs that you can easily carry or stick on your fridge as a reminder of your trip.

Christmas Decorations

During the holiday season, keep an eye out for Highland cow-themed Christmas ornaments and decorations. These festive souvenirs can bring a touch of Scottish cheer to your holiday celebrations.

Scottish Crafts

Explore local craft shops for handmade Scottish crafts like pottery, woodwork, and textiles. These unique and artisanal items reflect the craftsmanship and creativity of the region.

MUSEUMS AND GALLERIES

dinburgh is a city rich in history, culture, and the arts, and it's Ehome to numerous museums and galleries. Here are some notable ones you should consider visiting during your time in the city:

National Museum of Scotland

Located on Chambers Street, the National Museum of Scotland offers a fascinating journey through the country's history, culture, and natural world. Explore exhibits on Scottish history, archaeology, technology, and science. Don't miss the stunning Grand Gallery and the iconic Millennium Clock.

Scottish National Gallery

Situated on the Mound, the Scottish National Gallery houses an extensive collection of fine art, including works by renowned Scottish and international artists. Admire masterpieces from the Renaissance to the present day, including works by Van Gogh, Rembrandt, Turner, and Botticelli.

Museum of Edinburgh

Located on the Royal Mile, the Museum of Edinburgh showcases the city's rich history and heritage. Discover the story of Edinburgh through a variety of exhibits, including objects, artworks, and interactive displays that highlight the city's people, architecture, and traditions.

Scottish National Portrait Gallery

The Scottish National Portrait Gallery, situated on Queen Street, features an extensive collection of portraits of notable Scottish figures throughout history. Marvel at the diverse range of portraits, including those of monarchs, writers, inventors, and contemporary celebrities.

Museum of Childhood

The Museum of Childhood, located on the Royal Mile, offers a nostalgic journey through childhood memories. Explore toys, games, and artifacts from different eras, providing a glimpse into the lives of children in the past.

Surgeons' Hall Museums

Discover the fascinating history of surgery and medical science at the Surgeons' Hall Museums. Located near the Royal Mile, the museum houses collections of anatomical specimens, surgical instruments, and historical medical artifacts.

Scottish Parliament Visitor Centre

Learn about Scotland's devolved parliamentary system and the work of the Scottish Parliament at the Scottish Parliament Visitor Centre. Take a guided tour to explore the striking modern architecture and gain insights into Scottish politics and governance.

Museum of Edinburgh Writers' Museum

Situated in Lady Stair's House on the Royal Mile, the Writers' Museum celebrates the lives and works of renowned Scottish writers such as Robert Burns, Sir Walter Scott, and Robert Louis Stevenson. Discover manuscripts, books, and personal belongings of these literary figures.

Modern Art Galleries

Edinburgh is home to two modern art galleries. The Scottish National Gallery of Modern Art, located in a beautiful parkland setting, exhibits contemporary artworks and installations. The Fruitmarket Gallery, near Waverley Station, showcases cutting-edge contemporary art from both local and international artists.

The Real Mary King's Close: While not a traditional museum, The Real Mary King's Close offers a unique underground tour that takes you through a preserved network of narrow streets and houses beneath the Royal Mile. Discover the secrets and stories of Edinburgh's past.

WHISKY TASTING

hisky tasting is a popular activity in Edinburgh, given W Scotland's rich tradition and reputation for producing excellent whisky. Here's a guide to help you make the most of your whisky tasting experience in the city:

Whisky Bars and Pubs

Edinburgh has numerous whisky bars and pubs where you can sample a wide selection of whiskies. Some popular establishments include The Scotch Whisky Experience, The Bow Bar, The Devil's

Advocate, The Albanach, and Usquabae Whisky Bar & Larder. These venues offer knowledgeable staff, extensive whisky menus, and a cozy atmosphere to enjoy your tasting. Here are some notable whisky bars and pubs in Edinburgh:

The Scotch Whisky Experience

Located on the Royal Mile, near Edinburgh Castle, The Scotch Whisky Experience offers an extensive collection of whiskies from various regions of Scotland. They also provide whisky tastings and educational tours for whisky enthusiasts.

Usquabae Whisky Bar & Larder

Situated on Hope Street, Usquabae Whisky Bar & Larder is a haven for whisky enthusiasts seeking an exceptional tasting experience. With an extensive collection of over 400 whiskies from all regions of Scotland, this charming bar offers a delightful journey into the world of Scotland's national drink.

Upon entering Usquabae, you'll be enveloped in a warm and inviting ambiance that exudes the rich heritage and appreciation for whisky. The bar's cozy atmosphere, with its dim lighting and comfortable seating, sets the stage for a relaxed and immersive whisky tasting experience.

The highlight of Usquabae is undoubtedly its impressive whisky selection. The bar boasts a comprehensive range of single malts, blended whiskies, rare releases, and limited editions. Whisky connoisseurs and novices alike will find something to pique their interest as they peruse the extensive menu. From well-known distilleries to hidden gems, Usquabae caters to all palates and preferences.

What sets Usquabae apart is the knowledgeable staff who are passionate about whisky and eager to share their expertise. Whether you're a seasoned whisky enthusiast or new to the world of Scotch, the staff will guide you through the selection, offering insights into the flavors, aromas, and nuances of each whisky. Their recommendations and personalized service ensure that every visitor has a memorable and enjoyable experience.

In addition to its remarkable whisky collection, Usquabae also offers a larder of delectable Scottish fare. The menu features a range of traditional dishes made with locally sourced ingredients, designed to complement the whisky tasting experience. From artisanal cheeses and charcuterie to hearty Scottish classics, the larder offers a delectable array of flavors that harmonize with the complexity of the whiskies.

Usquabae's commitment to creating an immersive whisky experience extends beyond the bar itself. They also offer whisky tasting events and masterclasses, providing an opportunity to delve deeper into the world of whisky under the guidance of industry experts. These events offer a unique educational and sensory experience, allowing participants to further develop their appreciation for Scotland's liquid gold.

The Bon Vivant

Situated in the New Town on Thistle Street, The Bon Vivant is a stylish bar known for its exquisite cocktails, but it also offers an impressive selection of whiskies. It's a great place to enjoy a well-crafted drink in a sophisticated atmosphere.

The Bow Bar

Situated in the heart of the Old Town on Victoria Street, The Bow Bar is a traditional Scottish pub with a fantastic selection of whiskies. The cozy atmosphere and knowledgeable staff make it a favorite among whisky lovers.

The Devil's Advocate

This unique bar, nestled in an old Victorian pump house on Advocate's Close, boasts an impressive whisky selection alongside a diverse range of craft beers and cocktails. The Devil's Advocate also offers a delectable food menu featuring Scottish cuisine.

The Scotch Malt Whisky Society

Found on Queen Street, The Scotch Malt Whisky Society is a private members' club that opens its doors to non-members as well. They offer a wide range of unique and rare whiskies, often sourced directly from distilleries.

Whisky Tasting Events and Tours

Consider joining a whisky tasting event or tour in Edinburgh. Several companies offer guided experiences that take you through the process of whisky production, history, and tasting. The Scotch Whisky Experience on the Royal Mile, for example, provides interactive tours with the opportunity to sample different whiskies.

Whisky Distillery Tours

If you have the time, venture outside Edinburgh for a whisky distillery tour. There are several distilleries within driving distance, such as Glenkinchie, the closest distillery to Edinburgh, as well as The Macallan and Glenfiddich. These tours offer insights into the whisky-making process and often include tastings of their signature expressions. Here are some popular whisky distillery tours you can explore:

The Scotch Whisky Experience (Edinburgh)

While not a traditional distillery tour, The Scotch Whisky Experience in Edinburgh offers an interactive and educational tour that guides visitors through the whisky-making process. It includes a virtual whisky barrel ride, a sensory experience, and a chance to sample different whiskies.

Glenfiddich Distillery (Speyside)

Located in Dufftown, the Glenfiddich Distillery offers guided tours that take visitors through their whisky production process, including malting, mashing, fermentation, distillation, and maturation. The tour concludes with a tasting of their whiskies.

Talisker Distillery (Isle of Skye)

Situated on the Isle of Skye, the Talisker Distillery offers tours that allow visitors to witness the production of their distinctive and peaty single malt whisky. The tour includes a visit to the traditional worm tubs used in their distillation process and ends with a tasting.

Laphroaig Distillery (Islay)

Laphroaig, known for its heavily peated whiskies, provides visitors with an informative tour of their distillery on Islay. The tour offers a chance to explore their malting floors, peat kiln, and warehouses, and concludes with a tasting of their renowned whiskies.

Oban Distillery (Highland)

Located in the coastal town of Oban, the Oban Distillery offers guided tours that provide insights into their whisky production, including their unique small copper pot stills. The tour ends with a tasting of their whiskies.

Aberlour Distillery (Speyside)

Aberlour Distillery in Speyside offers tours that delve into their traditional whisky-making methods. Visitors can learn about their double cask maturation process and enjoy a tasting of their range of whiskies.

Whisky Tasting Flights

Many whisky bars and pubs offer tasting flights, which allow you to sample a range of whiskies in smaller quantities. These flights are usually curated by region, brand, or flavor profile, providing a comparative tasting experience.

Seek Guidance from Experts

If you're new to whisky tasting or want to expand your knowledge, don't hesitate to ask for recommendations or guidance from the staff or whisky experts. They can help you choose whiskies based on your preferences and provide insights into the different flavors, regions, and production methods.

Explore Different Whisky Regions

Scotland is divided into whisky-producing regions, each offering unique characteristics and flavor profiles. Some notable regions include Speyside, Highland, Islay, Lowland, and Campbeltown. Explore whiskies from different regions to appreciate the diversity and nuances of Scottish whisky. Here are the main whisky regions in Scotland:

Highland

The Highland region is the largest and most diverse whisky-producing region in Scotland. Highland whiskies can vary in flavor profiles, ranging from light and floral to rich and full-bodied.

Speyside

Located within the Highlands, Speyside is renowned for its concentration of distilleries and is considered a sub-region. Speyside whiskies are often characterized by their elegant and complex nature, with fruity, floral, and sometimes honeyed notes.

Islay

Islay is a small island on the west coast of Scotland and is famous for its heavily peated and smoky whiskies. Islay whiskies are often described as robust, medicinal, and briny, with distinct maritime characteristics.

Lowland

The Lowland region, located in the southern part of Scotland, is known for producing lighter and more gentle whiskies. Lowland whiskies are often characterized by their floral, grassy, and sometimes malty flavors.

Campbeltown

Campbeltown, situated on the Kintyre Peninsula, was once a prominent whisky region but now has only a few distilleries. Campbeltown whiskies are known for their distinctive maritime influence, along with a variety of flavors ranging from smoky to fruity.

Islands

The Islands region encompasses various islands, including Skye, Orkney, Mull, Jura, and Arran. While not officially recognized as a distinct whisky region, whiskies from these islands often exhibit their own unique characteristics, influenced by their coastal locations.

Note: It's important to note that while these regions provide a general guide to whisky styles, there can be variations within each region, and distilleries may produce whiskies that do not strictly adhere to regional characteristics. Exploring whiskies from different regions can be a fascinating journey, allowing whisky enthusiasts to appreciate the diversity and nuances of Scotland's national spirit.

Take Your Time

Whisky tasting is best enjoyed at a leisurely pace. Take your time to savor the aromas, flavors, and textures of each whisky. Observe the color, nose the glass to capture the scents, take small sips, and allow the whisky to linger on your palate. Water and palate-cleansing snacks like plain crackers or bread can help cleanse your palate between tastings.

Experiment with Pairings

Consider pairing your whiskies with complementary flavors. Dark chocolate, cheese, nuts, and smoked salmon are popular choices to enhance the tasting experience. Experiment with different pairings to find combinations that suit your preferences.

A LOVE AFFAIR WITH CANDY

f you have a sweet tooth and a love affair with candy, Edinburgh I offers plenty of delightful options to satisfy your cravings. Here are some recommendations for indulging in a candy-filled adventure:

Edinburgh Sweet Tours

Embark on a guided candy tour with Edinburgh Sweet Tours, where you can explore the city's sweet spots and learn about the history of candy. The tour includes visits to traditional sweet shops, sampling various confections, and discovering hidden gems.

Cuckoo's Bakery

Treat yourself to delicious cupcakes at Cuckoo's Bakery. With a rotating selection of flavors, you can enjoy tempting creations like Salted Caramel, Red Velvet, Lemon Meringue, and many more.

Cranachan & Crowdie

This charming little shop on the Royal Mile is a treasure trove of Scottish sweet treats. Indulge in traditional Scottish tablet (a crumbly fudge-like candy), handmade chocolates, toffees, and other confections made with local ingredients.

Fudge Kitchen

Visit Fudge Kitchen on the Royal Mile to experience the art of fudge-making. Watch as their skilled confectioners create delectable fudge using traditional methods and enjoy sampling their wide array of flavors, including classic vanilla, salted caramel, and rum 'n' raisin.

Lickety Splits

Located on Victoria Street, Lickety Splits is a delightful sweet shop filled with candies, chocolates, and nostalgic treats. Browse through their vast selection of pick 'n' mix sweets, retro candies, and international confections.

Miss Katie Cupcake

Visit Miss Katie Cupcake on Rose Street for a delightful assortment of cupcakes, brownies, and other sweet treats. Their beautifully decorated cupcakes come in a range of flavors, such as Oreo, Nutella, Raspberry Ripple, and many more.

Mary's Milk Bar

Located in the Grassmarket area, Mary's Milk Bar is renowned for its artisanal gelato and chocolates. Indulge in their delightful gelato flavors, such as Scottish Tablet, Rhubarb Crumble, and Dark Chocolate, or try their handcrafted chocolates for a decadent treat.

The Fudge House

Step into The Fudge House on the Royal Mile and be greeted by the heavenly aroma of freshly made fudge. Sample their mouthwatering selection of fudges, including traditional flavors like vanilla, chocolate, and butterscotch, as well as unique creations like whisky and ginger.

Sugar & Spice

Discover Sugar & Spice, a charming family-run sweet shop in Stockbridge. Explore shelves filled with old-fashioned candies, retro sweets, and international delights. It's a treasure trove for candy enthusiasts.

Hotel Chocolat

For luxurious chocolates and gourmet treats, visit Hotel Chocolat on Frederick Street. Explore their range of handcrafted chocolates, chocolate-covered fruits, truffles, and indulgent hot chocolates.

GHOST TOURS

dinburgh is famous for its rich history and haunting tales, Emaking it an ideal destination for ghost tours and paranormal enthusiasts. Here are some ghost tours in Edinburgh that offer a thrilling and spooky experience:

Mercat Tours

Mercat Tours offers ghost tours that delve into Edinburgh's dark past and supernatural legends. Choose from various themed tours, such as the Ghosts & Ghouls Tour, the Ghostly Underground Tour, or the Haunted Graveyard Tour.

The Witchery Ghosts & Gore Tour

For those seeking an adrenaline-inducing adventure into the paranormal, The Witchery Ghosts & Gore Tour is an experience not to be missed. Hosted by The Witchery by the Castle, a renowned restaurant and hotel in Edinburgh, this tour takes you on a spine-chilling journey through the city's haunted history, revealing tales of witches, ghosts, and other supernatural phenomena.

As night falls, you'll gather with fellow thrill -seekers to embark on this immersive and atmospheric tour. Led by expert guides well-versed in the city's dark folklore, you'll wander through narrow alleyways and hidden corners, delving into the eerie past of Edinburgh.

During the tour, you'll hear chilling tales of witchcraft, sorcery, and the infamous witch trials that once plagued the city. Learn about the real-life witches who were persecuted and condemned, their stories woven with historical facts and local legends. The guides will transport you back in time, painting a vivid picture of the trials and tribulations faced by those accused of witchcraft.

As you delve deeper into the tour, prepare to encounter ghostly tales and supernatural encounters. The guides will share hair-raising stories of spectral apparitions, restless spirits, and paranormal occurrences that are said to haunt Edinburgh's ancient streets and buildings. Brace yourself for tales of infamous haunted locations, where restless souls are rumored to wander in eternal unrest.

Throughout the tour, the guides create an immersive experience by sharing vivid descriptions, eerie sounds, and even demonstrating historical torture methods used during witch trials. Their storytelling prowess brings the haunted history of Edinburgh to life, evoking a sense of unease and fascination in equal measure.

The Witchery Ghosts & Gore Tour is not for the faint of heart, as it is designed to thrill and unsettle even the bravest souls. The tour aims to provide an authentic and spine-chilling experience, transporting participants into the dark underbelly of Edinburgh's supernatural realm.

Please note that due to the nature of the tour, it may not be suitable for young children or those who are easily frightened or sensitive to macabre themes.

City of the Dead Tours

City of the Dead Tours offers a variety of ghost tours, including the popular "Double Dead" tour that takes you through both the haunted Blair Street Underground Vaults and the Greyfriars Graveyard. Learn about the city's gruesome history and paranormal activity.

Auld Reekie Tours

Auld Reekie Tours offers a range of ghost tours that explore the haunted history of Edinburgh. From the Vaults & Graveyard Tour to the Ghosts & Ghouls Tour, these tours take you to eerie locations, including the Blair Street Underground Vaults and the Covenanters' Prison.

Haunted History Bus Tour

Hop aboard the Haunted History Bus Tour to explore Edinburgh's paranormal side. This immersive tour takes you to various haunted locations, sharing stories of ghostly sightings and unexplained phenomena.

The Edinburgh Dungeon

While not a traditional ghost tour, The Edinburgh Dungeon offers an interactive experience that combines history and dark storytelling. Prepare to be entertained by live actors as they bring to life Edinburgh's gruesome past, including tales of ghosts and infamous characters.

Supernatural Stories with Silent Disco

Silent Adventures offers a unique twist on ghost tours with their Supernatural Stories Silent Disco Tour. Put on your headphones, follow the guide, and enjoy ghostly tales and music as you explore the city.

DAY TRIPS FROM EDINBURGH

f you're looking to venture beyond Edinburgh and explore the I beautiful surrounding areas, there are several fantastic day trips you can take. Here are some popular destinations for day trips from Edinburgh:

Stirling Castle and the Trossachs

Visit Stirling Castle, a historic fortress that played a significant role in Scotland's history. Explore its grand halls and learn about its connections to Scottish royalty. Afterward, journey into the scenic Trossachs region, known as the "Highlands in Miniature," with its picturesque lochs, forests, and mountains.

Rosslyn Chapel and the Scottish Borders

Discover the mystical Rosslyn Chapel, famous for its intricate carvings and links to the Knights Templar and the Holy Grail legend. Combine your visit with a trip to the Scottish Borders, where you can explore quaint towns like Melrose, visit ancient abbeys, and enjoy the beautiful countryside.

Loch Ness and the Highlands

Take a day trip to the Highlands and immerse yourself in the breathtaking landscapes of Scotland. Visit Loch Ness, known for the mythical Loch Ness Monster, and enjoy the stunning scenery of mountains, glens, and lochs along the way.

St. Andrews

Explore the charming town of St. Andrews, known for its historic university, picturesque coastline, and world-famous golf courses. Visit the stunning ruins of St. Andrews Cathedral, wander along the beautiful beaches, and soak in the town's rich history and culture.

The Isle of Arran

Take a ferry from Ardrossan to the Isle of Arran and experience the natural beauty of "Scotland in Miniature." Enjoy the island's stunning landscapes, including mountains, beaches, and lochs. Visit Arran's distillery, explore castles, and discover its rich wildlife and hiking opportunities.

Falkland Palace and the East Neuk of Fife

A visit to Falkland Palace and the charming fishing villages of the East Neuk of Fife offers a delightful journey through history and picturesque landscapes.

Located in the town of Falkland, Falkland Palace is a magnificent Renaissance palace that holds a special place in Scottish history. Once a favorite residence of the Stuart kings and queens, the palace is steeped in regal grandeur and offers a fascinating glimpse into the lives of Scottish royalty.

As you explore Falkland Palace, you'll be captivated by its stunning architecture, ornate interiors, and well-preserved period features. Marvel at the intricately carved ceilings, admire the richly decorated rooms, and immerse yourself in the opulent ambiance of the past. The palace's beautifully landscaped gardens are equally enchanting, featuring elegant terraces, manicured lawns, and vibrant flower beds. Take a leisurely stroll through the gardens, soak in the serene atmosphere, and discover hidden corners that offer panoramic views of the surrounding countryside.

Beyond its architectural splendor, Falkland Palace also boasts a fascinating history. Learn about the Stuart dynasty and their connections to the palace, including Mary, Queen of Scots, who visited frequently during her reign. Discover stories of intrigue, power, and the rich cultural heritage that shaped Scotland's past.

After exploring Falkland Palace, venture into the East Neuk of Fife, a collection of picturesque fishing villages along the Fife coastline. Each village possesses its own unique charm and character, reflecting the area's rich maritime history.

Anstruther is a highlight of the East Neuk, known for its picturesque harbor and vibrant atmosphere. Take a leisurely stroll along the quayside, admire the colorful fishing boats, and indulge in freshly caught seafood from one of the local eateries. Don't miss the opportunity to visit the Scottish Fisheries Museum, where you can delve into the history and heritage of Scotland's fishing industry.

Crail is another enchanting village in the East Neuk. Its charming cobbled streets, historic buildings, and scenic harbor create a postcard-perfect setting. Explore the quaint shops, visit the Crail Museum and Heritage Centre, or simply enjoy the coastal views as you wander through the village.

Pittenweem, with its working harbor and bustling artist community, offers a unique blend of maritime heritage and artistic inspiration. Visit the galleries and studios, witness the vibrant arts scene, and soak up the village's captivating atmosphere.

The East Neuk of Fife is also known for its coastal walks, where you can enjoy breathtaking views of the rugged coastline, sandy beaches, and rolling hills. These walks offer an opportunity to connect with nature, breathe in the fresh sea air, and appreciate the unspoiled beauty of the area.

Culross and the Fife Coast

Visit the historic village of Culross, a beautifully preserved 16th-century town. Explore the cobbled streets, visit Culross Palace, and experience the atmosphere of a bygone era. Combine your trip with a scenic drive along the Fife Coast, stopping at charming coastal towns like Elie and Pittenweem.

The Scottish Borders and Abbotsford House

Embarking on a journey through the enchanting Scottish Borders region leads you to Abbotsford House, the former residence of the renowned Scottish writer Sir Walter Scott. Nestled along the banks of the River Tweed, this historic house offers a captivating glimpse into the life and literary legacy of one of Scotland's most beloved authors.

Approaching Abbotsford House, you'll be struck by its stunning architecture. The house reflects Scott's love for the Romantic style, featuring turrets, battlements, and intricate detailing. Step inside to explore the meticulously preserved rooms, each offering a window into the world of Scott and his literary inspirations.

The highlight of Abbotsford House is undoubtedly the extensive library, which showcases Scott's vast collection of books and manuscripts. Browse the shelves lined with literary treasures, including rare editions, historical documents, and personal correspondence. The library offers a unique opportunity to immerse yourself in the literary world that shaped Scott's imagination and influenced his writing.

As you wander through the house, you'll encounter rooms filled with artifacts and personal belongings, each revealing a different aspect of Scott's life. From the grand entrance hall to the elegant drawing rooms and the intimate study where he penned his literary masterpieces, Abbotsford House offers an intimate portrait of Scott's personal and creative pursuits.

Venturing outside, you'll discover the picturesque gardens that surround Abbotsford House. These meticulously landscaped grounds feature serene paths, vibrant flower beds, and tranquil water features, providing a tranquil retreat where you can relax and reflect on the beauty that inspired Scott. The gardens offer captivating views of the River Tweed, serving as a constant reminder of the landscape that influenced his writing.

Throughout your visit to Abbotsford House, informative exhibits and knowledgeable guides provide insights into Scott's life, literary works, and the historical context in which he lived. Whether you're a fan of his novels, poetry, or historical writings, or simply interested in the rich cultural heritage of Scotland, Abbotsford House offers a deep appreciation for Scott's contribution to literature and Scottish identity.

Beyond the house itself, the surrounding Scottish Borders region offers a wealth of natural beauty and historical sites to explore. From rolling hills and scenic valleys to ancient abbeys and charming market towns, the area is rich in both cultural heritage and breathtaking landscapes. Take the opportunity to immerse yourself in the history, folklore, and natural splendor of this enchanting region.

ART & CULTURE GUIDE

dinburgh is a vibrant city with a thriving arts and culture Escene. From world-class museums and galleries to festivals   and performances, there is something for everyone. Here's an art and culture guide to help you make the most of your visit to Edinburgh:

Festival City

Edinburgh is famous for its festivals. The Edinburgh Festival Fringe, the largest arts festival in the world, takes place annually in August, showcasing thousands of performances across all art forms. Additionally, the Edinburgh International Festival, the Edinburgh International Book Festival, and the Edinburgh International Film Festival are major cultural events worth experiencing.

The Edinburgh Festival Theatre

Catch a performance at the Edinburgh Festival Theatre, a major venue for theater, opera, and dance. It hosts a wide range of productions, including international touring shows, contemporary plays, and classical performances.

Royal Lyceum Theatre

Attend a play at the Royal Lyceum Theatre, one of Scotland's leading producing theaters. Known for its high-quality productions, it showcases a diverse range of dramas, comedies, and adaptations of classic works.

Traverse Theatre

The Traverse Theatre is renowned for promoting new and innovative works by emerging and established playwrights. Experience cutting-edge contemporary theater and performances that challenge and inspire.

Scottish Storytelling Centre

Immerse yourself in Scotland's rich oral storytelling tradition at the Scottish Storytelling Centre. Attend storytelling sessions, performances, and workshops that showcase the country's folklore, myths, and legends.

The Usher Hall

Lewis Noah

Enjoy a classical music concert or a performance by the Royal Scottish National Orchestra at the Usher Hall. This stunning venue is known for its exceptional acoustics and hosts a range of musical events throughout the year.

Filmhouse

Watch a diverse selection of films at Filmhouse, Edinburgh's premier independent cinema. It screens a mix of arthouse, classic, and international films, as well as hosting special events and film festivals.

Street Art and Murals

Edinburgh is not only renowned for its historic architecture but also for its vibrant street art scene. Exploring areas such as the Cowgate, Stockbridge, and Leith allows you to discover an array of impressive artworks that adorn buildings and walls throughout the city.

The Cowgate, located in the heart of the Old Town, is a bustling area known for its vibrant nightlife and alternative culture. As you wander through its winding streets, you'll encounter striking murals that add a splash of color and creativity to the urban landscape. These large-scale artworks, often showcasing a mix of styles and themes, captivate passersby and inject a sense of vibrancy into the historic surroundings.

Stockbridge, on the other hand, offers a more laid-back and bohemian atmosphere. This charming neighborhood is home to a variety of independent boutiques, cafes, and galleries. Amidst its quaint streets, you'll discover hidden gems of street art, often blending seamlessly with the neighborhood's artistic and creative character. From intricate stencil art to thought-provoking murals, the street art in Stockbridge adds an element of surprise and visual delight as you explore the area.

Leith, a vibrant port district with a rich maritime history, is another hotspot for street art enthusiasts. As you stroll along its waterfront, you'll encounter an impressive display of murals and graffiti that reflect the area's cultural diversity and creative energy. From large-scale murals paying homage to Leith's industrial heritage to colorful and expressive pieces that highlight social and political issues, the street art in Leith serves as a visual storyteller, inviting onlookers to engage with the local community and its narratives.

Edinburgh's street art scene is not limited to these specific areas. Throughout the city, you'll stumble upon art-filled alleys, hidden corners, and unexpected canvases that showcase the talents of both local and international artists. From iconic landmarks like the Elephant House, known for its association with J.K. Rowling and Harry Potter, to lesser-known nooks and crannies, Edinburgh's street art offers an ever -changing and dynamic canvas that reflects the city's evolving cultural landscape.

It's important to note that street art is an ephemeral art form, with artworks evolving and being replaced over time. What you see during your visit may differ from what others have experienced in the past, adding to the unique and transient nature of Edinburgh's street art scene.

CLASSES & WORKSHOPS

f you're looking to enhance your skills, learn something new, or I engage in a creative activity during your time in Edinburgh, the city offers a variety of classes and workshops. Here are some popular options to consider:

Art Classes

Unleash your creativity by joining art classes or workshops in Edinburgh. Various studios and art centers, such as the Edinburgh Drawing School and the Edinburgh Art School, offer classes in drawing, painting, sculpture, and other art forms. You can learn from experienced artists and instructors, regardless of your skill level.

Cooking and Baking Classes

Edinburgh has several cooking schools and culinary workshops where you can learn to prepare traditional Scottish dishes or explore international cuisines. Check out establishments like the Edinburgh New Town Cookery School or the Edinburgh School of Food and Wine for hands-on cooking experiences.

Photography Workshops

If you have an interest in photography, consider joining a photography workshop or tour in Edinburgh. Learn essential photography techniques, explore the city's picturesque locations, and capture stunning images with the guidance of professional photographers.

Whisky Tasting Masterclasses

Take your whisky appreciation to the next level by participating in whisky tasting masterclasses. The Scotch Whisky Experience and other whisky venues in the city offer expert-led workshops where you can learn about the production process, tasting notes, and the nuances of different whiskies.

Dance Classes

Experience the joy of movement by taking dance classes in Edinburgh. From ballet and contemporary dance to salsa and Scottish ceilidh dancing, you can find a range of classes suitable for various levels of experience. Dance Base and the Edinburgh Dance Academy are popular dance centers in the city.

Language Classes

If you're interested in learning a new language or improving your language skills, Edinburgh offers language schools and institutions where you can enroll in language classes. Whether you want to learn Scottish Gaelic, English as a second language, or another foreign language, you'll find options to suit your needs.

Yoga and Wellness Classes

Take a break from sightseeing and embrace relaxation and mindfulness by joining yoga and wellness classes in Edinburgh. Numerous studios and centers offer yoga, meditation, and wellness workshops, providing an opportunity to recharge and find inner balance.

Craft and DIY Workshops

Engage in hands-on creativity by participating in craft and DIY workshops in Edinburgh. Explore activities such as jewelry making, pottery, candle making, or woodworking. The Arienas Collective and the Red Thread Studio are known for their diverse craft workshops.

Music Lessons

If you're passionate about music, why not take music lessons during your stay in Edinburgh? Whether you want to learn to play a musical instrument, improve your singing skills, or explore music production, there are music schools and private tutors available to help you pursue your musical aspirations.

Fitness and Wellbeing Classes

Stay active and maintain your wellbeing by joining fitness and wellbeing classes in Edinburgh. From yoga and Pilates to high-intensity workouts and wellness retreats, the city offers a range of classes and activities to support your physical and mental wellbeing.

OUTDOOR ACTIVITIES

dinburgh's stunning natural surroundings and diverse E landscapes make it an excellent destination for outdoor enthusiasts. Whether you enjoy hiking, cycling, water sports, or simply immersing yourself in nature, there are plenty of outdoor

activities to enjoy. Here are some popular options:

Water of Leith Walkway

Follow the scenic Water of Leith Walkway, a picturesque riverside path that stretches from the city center to the port of Leith. Enjoy a leisurely walk or cycle along the path, passing through parks, woodlands, and historic sites.

Edinburgh's Beaches

Visit the nearby beaches, such as Portobello Beach or Cramond Beach, for a relaxing stroll, picnic, or even a dip in the sea during the summer months. Here are some beaches that are within a short distance from Edinburgh:

Portobello Beach

Located just a few miles east of the city center, Portobello Beach is the closest beach to Edinburgh. It stretches along the Firth of Forth and offers a sandy shoreline, a promenade, and various amenities such as cafes, ice cream shops, and a swimming pool.

Yellowcraig Beach

Situated in East Lothian, approximately 30 minutes east of Edinburgh by car, Yellowcraig Beach is known for its scenic beauty.

It features golden sands, dunes, and picturesque views of the Bass Rock and Firth of Forth. The area is also home to a nature reserve, making it a great spot for coastal walks and birdwatching.

Gullane Beach

Another beautiful beach in East Lothian, Gullane Beach is approximately a 40-minute drive east of Edinburgh. It offers a vast stretch of sandy shoreline, backed by dunes and grassy areas. The beach is popular for walking, picnicking, and enjoying panoramic views of the coastline.

North Berwick Beach

Located in the charming seaside town of North Berwick, around a 40-minute drive east of Edinburgh, this beach is a favorite among locals and visitors. With its expansive sandy beach, rock pools, and stunning views of the Bass Rock and Tantallon Castle, it's an ideal spot for coastal walks and family outings.

Pentland Hills Regional Park

Explore the Pentland Hills Regional Park, located just outside the city. This expansive park offers a range of outdoor activities, including hiking, mountain biking, horse riding, and wildlife spotting.

Water Sports in the Firth of Forth

Try your hand at various water sports in the Firth of Forth, such as kayaking, paddleboarding, or sailing. You can rent equipment and join guided tours from various locations along the coast.

Golf

Edinburgh and its surroundings boast numerous golf courses, including historic links courses like the Bruntsfield Links and Royal Burgess Golfing Society. Enjoy a round of golf surrounded by beautiful landscapes.

Bike Paths

Edinburgh has a network of cycling paths and routes that allow you to explore the city and its surroundings on two wheels. Rent a bike and pedal along paths like the Union Canal Towpath or the Innocent Railway Path.

Dalkeith Country Park

Dalkeith Country Park, located just south of Edinburgh, offers a delightful escape into nature, with its beautiful woodlands, riverside trails, and a range of exciting activities for all ages. Whether you're a nature lover, adventure seeker, or history enthusiast, Dalkeith Country Park has something to offer.

As you enter the park, you'll be greeted by a picturesque landscape that encompasses woodlands, meadows, and a meandering river. The park boasts an extensive network of walking and cycling trails, allowing you to explore its natural beauty at your own pace. Take a leisurely stroll along the riverside, breathe in the fresh air, and immerse yourself in the tranquility of the surroundings.

For those seeking a thrilling experience, Dalkeith Country Park offers tree -top adventures through the acclaimed "Go Ape" course. Strap on a harness, navigate high ropes, and zip-line through the tree canopy, taking in breathtaking views from above. This exhilarating activity is suitable for both children and adults, providing an unforgettable adventure amidst the park's lush greenery.

Nature enthusiasts will appreciate the park's rich biodiversity and wildlife. Keep your eyes peeled for a variety of bird species, including herons, kingfishers, and woodpeckers, as well as squirrels and other small mammals that call the park home. The park's natural habitats provide ample opportunities for wildlife spotting and birdwatching.

Dalkeith Country Park is also steeped in history, with several historic attractions to explore. The centerpiece is Dalkeith Palace, an impressive mansion that dates back to the 17th century. While the palace itself is not open to the public, you can admire its grand architecture and learn about its fascinating history from the exterior. The park also features the restored 18th-century stableyard, which now houses shops, cafes, and a visitor center where you can gather information about the park's attractions and activities.

Throughout the year, Dalkeith Country Park hosts a variety of events, including outdoor concerts, craft fairs, and seasonal festivities. Check the park's website or local listings to see if there are any special events happening during your visit.

Wildlife Watching

Scotland's rich and diverse wildlife is a treat for nature enthusiasts. To fully immerse yourself in the country's natural wonders, joining wildlife tours or visiting nature reserves is an excellent way to spot a variety of birds, seals, and other fascinating creatures in their natural habitats. Here are a couple of notable locations to consider:

RSPB Scotland Loch Leven

Located in Kinross, RSPB Scotland Loch Leven is a beautiful nature reserve that encompasses a large freshwater loch surrounded by woodlands and wetlands. The reserve is home to a wide range of bird species, making it a birdwatcher's paradise. From the comfort of bird hides, you can observe resident and migratory birds, including ospreys, pink-footed geese, and various waterfowl. The reserve also offers walking trails, allowing you to explore the diverse habitats and enjoy the tranquility of the surroundings.

Scottish Seabird Centre

Situated in North Berwick, the Scottish Seabird Centre offers a captivating opportunity to observe seabird colonies and marine wildlife along the spectacular East Lothian coastline. Take a boat trip to the nearby Bass Rock, a volcanic island renowned for its massive gannet colony. The sight and sound of thousands of gannets nesting on the cliffs is truly awe-inspiring. The Scottish Seabird Centre itself features interactive exhibits, live webcams, and expert guides who can provide insights into the behavior and ecology of the seabirds.

Apart from these locations, Scotland has numerous other nature reserves, national parks, and wildlife centers where you can witness the country's incredible biodiversity. From the Cairngorms National Park with its majestic landscapes and rare wildlife, to the Isle of Mull known for its sea eagles and otters, each destination offers unique wildlife encounters.

Remember to check the timings and availability of guided tours, boat trips, or any specific activities offered at these locations, as they may vary depending on the season. Additionally, be respectful of the wildlife and follow any guidelines or regulations in place to ensure their well-being and conservation.

Edinburgh Botanic Garden

When seeking tranquility amidst the vibrant city of Edinburgh, the Edinburgh Botanic Garden provides a serene oasis. This peaceful haven offers a delightful escape where you can stroll through beautiful gardens, explore glasshouses, and immerse yourself in the seasonal displays of flowers and plants.

As you enter the Edinburgh Botanic Garden, you'll be greeted by lush green spaces and meticulously manicured landscapes. The gardens feature a diverse collection of plants, both native and exotic, arranged in themed areas that showcase different botanical habitats. Take a leisurely walk along winding paths, surrounded by vibrant flower beds, aromatic herbs, and towering trees. Discover hidden corners, secluded benches, and peaceful ponds, where you can relax and rejuvenate amidst nature's tranquility.

One of the highlights of the Edinburgh Botanic Garden is its collection of glasshouses. Step inside these magnificent structures and explore a world of tropical rainforests, arid desert landscapes, and exotic plant species. The glasshouses provide an immersive experience, allowing you to witness plant life from various corners of the globe, all within the confines of this botanical sanctuary.

Throughout the year, the Edinburgh Botanic Garden showcases a variety of seasonal displays that captivate visitors with their beauty and fragrance. From vibrant spring blooms to stunning summer floral arrangements, the garden's ever-changing palette offers a feast for the senses. During autumn, witness the transformation of foliage into a kaleidoscope of warm hues, while winter brings its own charm with displays of festive lights and evergreens.

Aside from its natural beauty, the Edinburgh Botanic Garden also hosts educational programs, workshops, and exhibitions that cater to visitors of all ages. Learn about horticulture, conservation, and the importance of plants in our ecosystem through interactive displays and guided tours. Engage with knowledgeable staff and experts who are passionate about sharing their botanical knowledge and fostering a love for nature.

The garden also features a café where you can enjoy a cup of tea or a light meal amidst the tranquil surroundings. Savor the flavors of locally sourced ingredients while admiring the views of the garden's landscape.

SEASONAL & SPECIAL OCCASIONS

dinburgh hosts several seasonal and special occasions E throughout the year, adding to the city's vibrant atmosphere and providing unique experiences for visitors. Here are some notable seasonal events and special occasions in Edinburgh:

Edinburgh Festival Fringe (August)

The Edinburgh Festival Fringe is the largest arts festival in the world, featuring thousands of performances across various art forms, including theater, comedy, dance, music, and more. The city comes alive with street performances, pop-up venues, and a lively atmosphere.

Edinburgh International Festival (August)

The Edinburgh International Festival runs alongside the Fringe and showcases a range of high-quality artistic performances, including classical music concerts, theater productions, opera, and dance performances.

Edinburgh's Hogmanay (New Year's Eve)

Edinburgh's Hogmanay is a world-famous New Year's celebration, attracting visitors from around the globe. Festivities include a torchlight procession, street parties, live music, fireworks, and the traditional "Loony Dook" swim in the freezing waters of the River Forth on New Year's Day.

Christmas Markets (November-December)

During the festive season, Edinburgh is adorned with Christmas decorations and hosts several Christmas markets. The popular markets, such as the European Christmas Market in Princes Street Gardens and the Scottish Market on George Street, offer a range of festive goods, food, drinks, and entertainment.

Beltane Fire Festival (April)

The Beltane Fire Festival is a unique celebration of the arrival of summer. Held on Calton Hill, it involves vibrant processions, fire performances, and dramatic rituals inspired by ancient Celtic traditions.

Edinburgh International Book Festival (August)

Book lovers can enjoy the Edinburgh International Book Festival, where renowned authors and emerging writers gather to discuss their works, participate in readings, and engage in literary discussions.

Royal Highland Show (June)

The Royal Highland Show, held at the Royal Highland Centre, showcases Scotland's rural traditions, agriculture, livestock shows, and equestrian events. It's an excellent opportunity to experience Scottish farming culture.

Burns Night (January 25th)

Celebrate the life and works of Scotland's national poet, Robert Burns, on Burns Night. Traditional events include Burns Suppers, featuring haggis, poetry recitations, bagpipe music, and Scottish dancing.

Easter Weekend

Edinburgh celebrates Easter with various events, including egg hunts, family-friendly activities, and special Easter-themed exhibitions and performances at museums and attractions.

Edinburgh Marathon Festival (May)

The Edinburgh Marathon Festival is a weekend-long event that includes races for all ages and abilities, from a full marathon to shorter distances. Participants run through the city's iconic landmarks, providing a unique way to explore Edinburgh.

TICKETS & PASSES

hen visiting Edinburgh, it's helpful to know about various W ticket options and passes that can enhance your experience and save you money. Here are some ticket and pass options to consider:

Edinburgh City Pass

The Edinburgh City Pass offers access to multiple attractions and includes free transportation to and from the airport. It provides entry to popular sites like Edinburgh Castle, the Royal Yacht Britannia, and the Palace of Holyroodhouse, among others. It's available for different durations (1, 2, or 3 days) and can be a cost-effective option if you plan to visit multiple attractions.

Historic Scotland Explorer Pass

If you're interested in exploring historic sites and castles, consider the Historic Scotland Explorer Pass. It grants access to over 70 attractions across Scotland, including Edinburgh Castle, Stirling Castle, and Urquhart Castle. The pass is available for different durations (3, 7, or 14 days) and allows you to visit multiple sites at your own pace.

Royal Edinburgh Ticket

The Royal Edinburgh Ticket combines admission to three iconic attractions in Edinburgh: Edinburgh Castle, the Palace of Holyroodhouse, and the Royal Yacht Britannia. It also includes unlimited travel on the hop-on hop-off sightseeing buses for 48 hours.

Festival and Event Tickets

If you're planning to attend specific festivals or events, such as the Edinburgh Festival Fringe or the Edinburgh International Festival, it's advisable to book tickets in advance. Many events offer early bird discounts or package deals for multiple shows.

Individual Attraction Tickets

For individual attractions like Edinburgh Castle, the Palace of Holyroodhouse, or the Scotch Whisky Experience, you can purchase tickets directly at the entrance or online. Booking online in advance can sometimes offer discounted rates and allow you to skip the ticket queues.

Public Transportation Tickets

To get around Edinburgh, you can purchase single tickets for buses or trams directly from the driver or use contactless payment methods. Alternatively, you can consider purchasing a day ticket or a multi-day Lothian Buses Ridacard, which offers unlimited travel on buses and trams within specified zones.

Guided Tour Tickets

If you're interested in guided tours, such as ghost tours, walking tours, or themed tours, it's best to book tickets in advance to secure your spot. Many tour companies have online booking systems or physical ticket offices in popular areas.

UNIQUE EXPERIENCES

dinburgh offers a range of unique experiences that can make E your visit to the city truly memorable. Here are some special and distinctive activities to consider:

Royal Edinburgh Military Tattoo

Experience the world-renowned Royal Edinburgh Military Tattoo, a spectacular event held annually on the esplanade of Edinburgh Castle. Enjoy a mesmerizing display of military bands, bagpipes, drummers, and dancers against the backdrop of the castle.

Underground Vaults Tour

Explore the mysterious underground vaults beneath the streets of Edinburgh. Join a guided tour to learn about their history, including their use as storage spaces, illicit activities, and rumored paranormal activity. It's a fascinating and sometimes eerie journey into the city's hidden past.

Climb Calton Hill for Sunrise or Sunset

Calton Hill offers panoramic views of the city and is an ideal spot to watch the sunrise or sunset. Climb to the top and enjoy breathtaking vistas of Edinburgh's iconic landmarks, such as Edinburgh Castle and Arthur's Seat, bathed in the golden light of dawn or dusk.

Camera Obscura and World of Illusions

Visit Camera Obscura and World of Illusions, a unique attraction that combines optical illusions, interactive exhibits, and mind-boggling displays. Discover the wonders of perception, light, and visual trickery as you explore this interactive museum.

Real Mary King's Close

Take a guided tour through Real Mary King's Close, an underground warren of narrow streets and hidden passages beneath the Royal Mile. Learn about the life and times of the people who lived in these preserved 17th-century streets and hear their fascinating stories.

Holyrood Park by Horseback

Experience the beauty of Holyrood Park on horseback. Join a guided horse riding tour that takes you through this scenic park, offering breathtaking views of Arthur's Seat, Salisbury Crags, and the city skyline.

Ghost Tours and Paranormal Experiences

Edinburgh's rich history and tales of paranormal activity make it a perfect city for ghost tours and paranormal experiences. Join a guided ghost tour, explore haunted locations, or even participate in paranormal investigations to uncover the city's supernatural secrets.

Literary Pub Tour

Embark on a literary pub tour and follow in the footsteps of famous Scottish writers. Enjoy a blend of storytelling, theater, and pub culture as your guides entertain you with tales of Edinburgh's literary history and take you to traditional pubs associated with renowned authors.

Traditional Scottish Ceilidh

Attend a traditional Scottish ceilidh, a social gathering with live music and lively dancing. Join in the energetic dances, guided by experienced ceilidh callers, and immerse yourself in Scottish culture and traditional music.

The Scotch Whisky Experience

Dive into the world of Scotch whisky at The Scotch Whisky Experience. Take a guided tour to learn about the whisky-making process, explore a vast collection of whiskies, and participate in a tasting session to savor the distinct flavors and aromas of this iconic Scottish spirit.

HIDDEN GEMS

St. Anthony's Chapel Ruins

St. Anthony's Chapel was a medieval chapel that dates back to the 15th century. It was originally built by the Guild of St. Anthony, an organization that cared for the sick and those affected by the plague. The chapel was dedicated to St. Anthony, the patron saint of those suffering from infectious diseases.

The ruins of St. Anthony's Chapel are situated on a rocky outcrop in Holyrood Park, just east of the city center. The park offers stunning views of Edinburgh and is a popular recreational area for locals and visitors.

Today, only the remains of St. Anthony's Chapel stand, with the structure mostly reduced to its foundations and some remnants of the walls. The site provides a glimpse into the architectural style and construction methods of the medieval period.

Visiting St. Anthony's Chapel Ruins provides an opportunity to connect with Edinburgh's medieval history and enjoy the natural beauty of Holyrood Park. The site offers a tranquil setting away from the bustle of the city, allowing visitors to appreciate the remnants of this ancient place of worship.

The Canongate Tolbooth

The Canongate Tolbooth is a historic building located on the Royal Mile in Edinburgh's Old Town. It is a significant architectural and historical landmark in the city. The Canongate Tolbooth was built in 1591 and served as a town hall and administrative center for the burgh of Canongate, which was a separate town located outside the walls of Edinburgh. It was used for various civic purposes, including council meetings, courts, and public gatherings.

The Canongate Tolbooth is an impressive example of Scottish Renaissance architecture. It features distinctive crowstepped gables, a clock tower, and an ornate facade adorned with carved details. The building's design reflects the prosperity and importance of the Canongate burgh during the 16th century.

Throughout its history, the Canongate Tolbooth has served multiple functions. In addition to its administrative role, it also housed a prison, with cells in the basement where prisoners were held. The building also contained shops and markets on the ground floor.

Today, the Canongate Tolbooth is part of the Museum of Edinburgh, which is operated by the City of Edinburgh Council. The museum showcases the history and culture of Edinburgh, including exhibits on the Canongate area and the city's development over time. Visitors can explore the building's historical spaces and learn about its significance in the city's history.

Visiting the Canongate Tolbooth and the Museum of Edinburgh provides an opportunity to step back in time and learn about the rich history of Edinburgh's Old Town. The building's striking architecture and its role in the city's civic life make it a significant landmark worth exploring during your visit to Edinburgh.

Dr Neil's Garden

Located on the shores of Duddingston Loch, near Arthur's Seat, Dr Neil's Garden is a serene and beautifully landscaped garden. It's a hidden gem that offers a peaceful escape from the city, with stunning views, lush greenery, and a variety of flowers and plants.

The Writers' Museum

Tucked away on Lady Stair's Close, just off the Royal Mile, the Writers' Museum pays tribute to Scotland's literary heritage. This small museum celebrates the lives and works of famous Scottish writers such as Robert Burns, Sir Walter Scott, and Robert Louis Stevenson.

Craigmillar Castle

Often overshadowed by its more famous counterpart, Edinburgh Castle, Craigmillar Castle is a well-preserved medieval fortress located on the outskirts of the city. It offers a quieter and more atmospheric experience, allowing visitors to explore its towers, courtyards, and a beautiful view of the surrounding landscape.

St. Bernard's Well

Nestled in the Dean Village area, St. Bernard's Well is a hidden neoclassical structure dedicated to the healing properties of the nearby mineral spring. The well features a stunning temple-like design and offers a tranquil spot to relax and enjoy the scenic views of the Water of Leith.

BEST CASTLES YOU CAN STAY IN

Here are a few notable castles near Edinburgh that provide accommodation options:

Dalhousie Castle

Located about 8 miles southeast of Edinburgh, Dalhousie Castle is a 13th-century fortress that has been converted into a luxury hotel. It offers elegant rooms, fine dining, and a spa. Staying at Dalhousie Castle allows you to immerse yourself in the history and grandeur of a Scottish castle while enjoying modern comforts.

Dundas Castle

Situated about 8 miles west of Edinburgh, Dundas Castle is a stunning 15th-century castle that has been transformed into an exclusive-use venue and luxury accommodation. It offers a range of luxurious suites and cottages, along with beautiful grounds and event facilities. Staying at Dundas Castle provides a unique and intimate castle experience.

Carberry Tower

Located about 9 miles east of Edinburgh, Carberry Tower is a grand 16th-century castle set in beautiful parkland. It offers luxurious accommodations, exquisite dining, and picturesque surroundings. Carberry Tower combines historic charm with modern comforts.

Melville Castle

Situated about 8 miles southeast of Edinburgh, Melville Castle is an 18th-century castle hotel set within a sprawling estate. It offers stylish rooms, a bar, and a restaurant, allowing you to experience a taste of castle living. The castle's elegant architecture and serene setting provide a tranquil retreat.

ITINERARIES

Classic Edinburgh Highlights (2 days)

Day 1: Visit Edinburgh Castle, stroll down the Royal Mile, explore the Palace of Holyroodhouse, and hike up Arthur's Seat for panoramic views.

Day 2: Take a tour of the Royal Yacht Britannia, wander through the picturesque Dean Village, visit the National Museum of Scotland, and enjoy an evening ghost tour.

Edinburgh for History Buffs (3 days)

Day 1: Explore the Old Town, including Edinburgh Castle, the Real Mary King's Close, and the Museum of Edinburgh.

Day 2: Visit the National Museum of Scotland, the Surgeons' Hall Museum, and the Writers' Museum. Take a guided historical walking tour.

Day 3: Journey to the outskirts of the city to see Rosslyn Chapel, explore the historic village of South Queensferry, and visit the Forth Bridge.

Whisky and Scottish Heritage (4 days)

Day 1: Explore the Scotch Whisky Experience and take a tour of the historic Glenkinchie Distillery.

Day 2: Visit Stirling Castle and the Wallace Monument. Stop by the Glengoyne Distillery on the way back to Edinburgh.

Day 3: Take a day trip to the Scottish Borders to visit Melrose Abbey, Abbotsford House, and the Tweed Valley.

Day 4: Discover the secrets of the Royal Mile Whiskies, enjoy a tasting at the Bow Bar, and explore the historic pubs of Edinburgh.

Family-Friendly Edinburgh (3 days)

Day 1: Visit the National Museum of Scotland and Dynamic Earth. Take a walk through Holyrood Park.

Day 2: Explore Edinburgh Zoo, climb aboard the Royal Yacht Britannia, and visit Camera Obscura.

Day 3: Spend the day at the Royal Botanic Garden, enjoy a picnic in Princes Street Gardens, and take a ride on the Ferris wheel at the Christmas Market (seasonal).

Art and Culture Tour (2 days)

Day 1: Visit the Scottish National Gallery, the Scottish National Portrait Gallery, and the Museum of Edinburgh.

Day 2: Explore the Scottish Parliament, take a guided tour of the Scottish Opera or National Theatre of Scotland, and catch a show at the Edinburgh Festival Theatre.

Outdoor Adventures in Edinburgh (3 days)

Day 1: Hike up Arthur's Seat, explore the Royal Botanic Garden, and take a bike ride along the Water of Leith.

Day 2: Visit the Edinburgh International Climbing Arena, try your hand at indoor bouldering, and go kayaking on the Union Canal.

Day 3: Take a day trip to the Pentland Hills for hiking and enjoy a scenic drive to the picturesque village of South Queensferry.

Literary Edinburgh (2 days)

Day 1: Visit the Writers' Museum, the Scott Monument, and Greyfriars Kirkyard (inspiration for Harry Potter). Attend a literary event if available.

Day 2: Explore the locations associated with Sir Walter Scott, such as Abbotsford House and Scott Monument. Visit the Museum of Edinburgh.

Hidden Gems of Edinburgh (3 days):

Day 1: Discover the charm of Dean Village, explore the secret gardens of Dunbar's Close, and visit the underground Mary King's Close.

Day 2: Explore the charming neighborhood of Stockbridge, visit the Museum of Childhood, and wander through the Botanic Cottage.

Day 3: Discover the secret gardens of Dr Neil's Garden, visit the quirky Surgeons' Hall Museums, and explore the historic Leith area.

Food and Drink Tour of Edinburgh (2 days)

Day 1: Explore the vibrant food markets like the Edinburgh Farmers' Market and Stockbridge Market. Visit local pubs and sample traditional Scottish dishes.

Day 2: Take a whiskey tasting tour, visit local breweries and distilleries, and indulge in a gourmet dinner at a Michelin-starred restaurant.

Edinburgh Festival Fringe (5 days)

Day 1:

Morning: Arrive in Edinburgh and check into your accommodation.

Afternoon: Familiarize yourself with the city by taking a walking tour of the Old Town. Explore the Royal Mile, visit the iconic Edinburgh Castle, and soak in the lively festival atmosphere.

Evening: Attend your first Fringe show! Pick a comedy, theater, or music performance based on your interests. Check the festival program or website for a wide range of options.

Day 2:

Morning: Start the day with a visit to the Fringe Box Office to browse the program and get information about upcoming shows. Grab a quick breakfast at a local café.

Afternoon: Spend the afternoon exploring different festival venues and street performances throughout the city. Take in the bustling atmosphere and enjoy the vibrant street entertainment.

Evening: Attend a stand-up comedy show or a theater performance at one of the many venues. Consider booking tickets in advance for popular acts or shows that you're particularly interested in.

Day 3:

Morning: Take a break from the festival and explore other attractions in Edinburgh. Visit the National Museum of Scotland, stroll through the beautiful Princes Street Gardens, or climb Calton Hill for panoramic views of the city.

Afternoon: Explore the art exhibitions and installations that are part of the festival. The Fringe showcases a variety of visual arts, including photography, paintings, and sculptures.

Evening: Immerse yourself in the festival atmosphere by attending a late-night cabaret or variety show. These performances often feature a mix of comedy, music, and acrobatics.

Day 4:

Morning: Start the day with a relaxing walk along the Water of Leith, an enchanting river walkway that winds through the city. Enjoy the tranquility before diving back into the festival excitement.

Afternoon: Attend a workshop or participate in a creative event offered by the festival. These interactive sessions provide a hands-on experience and a chance to learn from professionals in various artistic fields.

Evening: Wrap up your festival experience by attending a grand finale or closing show. These performances often feature spectacular acts and bring the festival to a memorable conclusion.

Day 5:

Morning: Take a leisurely breakfast and reflect on your festival experience. Share your favorite shows and highlights with friends or fellow festival-goers.

Afternoon: Visit the Edinburgh Festival Fringe Shop to browse and purchase festival merchandise as souvenirs. You can find T-shirts, tote bags, and other memorabilia to remember your time at the Fringe.

Evening: Enjoy a farewell dinner at a local restaurant, perhaps with some traditional Scottish dishes. Raise a glass to your fantastic Edinburgh Festival Fringe adventure!

MAPS

Scotland Map

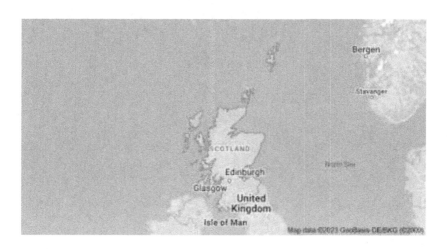

Edinburgh Map

Cycle Map

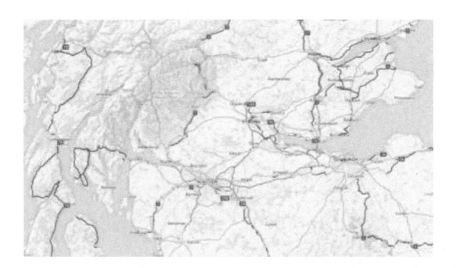

Restaurants Map

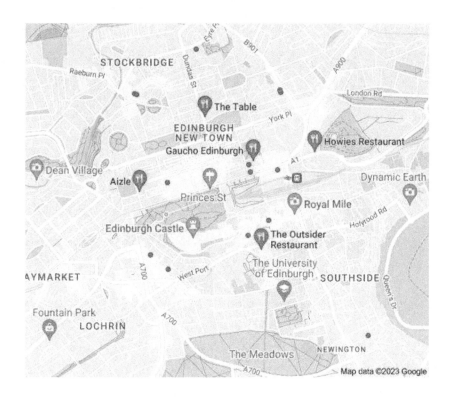

Edinburgh Attractions Map

FAQ

What are the Top 10 sights in Edinburgh?

Edinburgh's main attractions lie on the Royal Mile, with the impressive castle on one side and the palace of Holyroodhouse on the other side of the Royal Mile. Other highlights include the Royal Yacht Britannia, Calton Hill, Arthur's Seat, Greyfriars Bobby's cemetery and the dark side of Edinburgh in the Underground Vaults. In this article you can read all about the Top 20 Edinburgh Sightseeing.

Can I visit the castle for free?

No, without tickets you can only view the castle from the outside. You must buy tickets to visit the castle, including the rooms and exhibitions. More info about Edinburgh Castle tickets.

What are fun activities in Edinburgh?

The best tours in Edinburgh all have to do with the dark side of the city. Visit Greyfriars graveyard at night or go underground at The Real Mary King's Close or at the Underground Vaults. You can take a fun Harry Potter tour with children and whiskey enthusiasts can visit the Whiskey Experience. More info about Edinburgh activities.

What museums does the Scottish capital have?

The most famous museum is the National Museum of Scotland, which can be visited for free. Other popular museums include The World of Illusions with the Camera Obscura, the Scottish National Gallery and numerous small museums on the Royal Mile. In this article you can read all about the Museums in Edinburgh.

CONCLUSIONS

dinburgh is a city that captivates visitors with its rich history, Estunning architecture, vibrant culture, and natural beauty.

This travel guide has provided you with an overview of the must-visit attractions, cultural experiences, and day trips that await you in this enchanting Scottish city. Whether you're interested in exploring the historical landmarks, immersing yourself in the city's festivals, or embarking on scenic adventures to the Scottish Highlands, Edinburgh offers a diverse range of experiences that will leave a lasting impression. So, start planning your trip to Edinburgh and get ready for an unforgettable journey through the heart of Scotland!

INDEX

Printed in Great Britain
by Amazon